THE ULTIMATE BIBLE
SCRAMBLE BOOK

Put Your Brainpower to the Test

KEN SAVE

BARBOUR
PUBLISHING

ISBN 1-58660-974-2

Published by Barbour Publishing, Inc., P.O. Box 719, Uhrichsville, Ohio 44683, www.barbourbooks.com

Printed in the United States of America.
5 4 3 2 1

THE ULTIMATE BIBLE
SCRAMBLE BOOK

DIRECTIONS

SCRAMBLED CIRCLES PUZZLES

Unscramble the words from the list provided, placing the corrected words in the numbered blanks. Then use the circled letters to answer the question that follows.

Prolonging Your Life

1. CBMEREA
2. IMDWOS
3. LWNGEKODE
4. TMESEE
5. PTRISI
6. GITHS
7. RYASE
8. SRTEPNE
9. ETDPH
10. CEALP

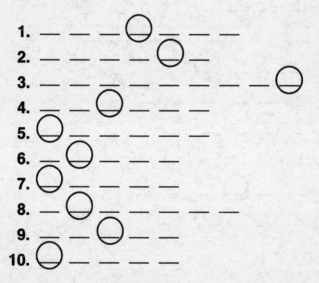

Keeping God's commands will prolong your life and bring ⬯⬯⬯⬯⬯⬯⬯⬯⬯⬯.

(Job 22:21)

Leaving the Pyramids Behind

1. **ISEVRP**
2. **ESTLSANIS**
3. **RRBTEHO**
4. **ATLPMER**
5. **NAVEHE**
6. **DTSERE**
7. **ANNRWGI**
8. **REZFEE**

1. __ __ __ __ Ⓞ __

2. __ Ⓞ __ __ __ __ __ __ __

3. __ __ __ Ⓞ __ __

4. __ __ __ __ __ __ Ⓞ

5. __ __ Ⓞ __ __ __

6. __ __ __ __ Ⓞ

7. __ __ __ Ⓞ __ __ __

8. __ __ __ Ⓞ __

It was a new home after Egypt.

Ⓞ Ⓞ Ⓞ Ⓞ Ⓞ Ⓞ Ⓞ Ⓞ

(Matthew 2:22–23)

8

Too Bland!

___

1. **UEDJG**
2. **RDSENKAS**
3. **NWRROA**
4. **ADWERSR**
5. **EDAVRSARY**
6. **NAFTIGS**
7. **GLLAE**
8. **FOREFIC**

1. — — — — ⊖
2. — ⊖ — — — — — ⊖
3. ⊖ — — — — —
4. — — — — — — ⊖
5. — — — — ⊖ — — —
6. — — — ⊖ — — —
7. ⊖ — — — —
8. — — — ⊖ — — —

Once this is lost, it's not good for anything.

⊖⊖⊖⊖⊖⊖⊖⊖⊖

(Matthew 5:13)

Interesting Names

1. CMROPALI
2. LIRAJE
3. RVCIPENO
4. NBTIAHI
5. SMCUOT

6. RRUPOA
7. RVETLA
8. LTEFE
9. ECUFRAL

1. Ⓞ _ _ _ _ _ _ _

2. _ _ Ⓞ _ _ _

3. _ _ _ _ Ⓞ _ _ _

4. _ _ _ Ⓞ _ _ _

5. _ _ _ Ⓞ _

6. _ _ _ Ⓞ _ _

7. _ _ Ⓞ _ _ _

8. _ Ⓞ _ _ _

9. _ _ _ _ _ _ Ⓞ

"When they had passed through Amphipolis and Ⓞ Ⓞ Ⓞ Ⓞ Ⓞ Ⓞ Ⓞ Ⓞ, they came to Thessalonica, where there was a Jewish synagogue."

(Acts 17:1)

Unto Death

1. **CRCDFIEIU**
2. **TFHAI**
3. **TNAELER**
4. **ARUTNE**
5. **ANICSERE**
6. **TBMSAPI**
7. **OLRCTON**
8. **WEGSA**

1. _ _ _ _ _ Ⓞ _ _

2. _ Ⓞ _ _ _

3. _ _ Ⓞ _ _ _ _ _

4. _ Ⓞ _ _ _ _ _

5. _ _ _ Ⓞ _ _ _ _

6. _ _ _ _ _ Ⓞ _

7. _ _ _ _ Ⓞ _ _

8. _ _ Ⓞ _ _

Death is the release from

Ⓞ Ⓞ Ⓞ Ⓞ Ⓞ Ⓞ Ⓞ .

(Romans 7:2)

Deaf Ears

1. OANMRS
2. RRVWTEOHO
3. BEKEUR
4. EPTCRES
5. NCWSEIKSDE
6. TDUNREP

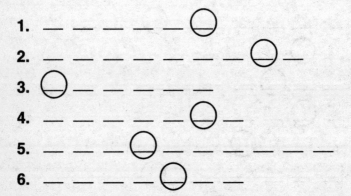

1. _ _ _ _ _ ⊖ _
2. _ _ _ _ _ _ _ ⊖ _
3. ⊖ _ _ _ _ _
4. _ _ _ _ ⊖ _
5. _ _ _ ⊖ _ _ _ _ _
6. _ _ _ _ ⊖ _ _

A ⊖⊖⊖⊖⊖⊖ never listens to instruction or advice.

(Proverbs 15:12)

Few but Proud!

1. **OENGERSU**
2. **PPTIRONOOR**
3. **CEGANUREO**
4. **KBEORN**
5. **DBNTSOIEDEI**
6. **RCCDOA**
7. **HESFMIL**

1. _ _ _◯_ _ _ _
2. _ _ _ _◯_ _ _ _
3. _◯_ _ _ _ _ _
4. _ _ _ _◯_
5. _ _ _ _ _ _ _ _ _ _◯
6. ◯_ _ _ _ _
7. _ _◯_ _ _ _

This is left by God's choice.

(Ezra 9:8)

An Honest Mirror

1. **CNDNEATESD**
2. **SPAEGAS**
3. **SAENCD**
4. **AGTDFRE**
5. **ECUFHLRE**
6. **SEJHOP**
7. **VROGEN**
8. **TOMUH**

1. _ _ _ _ _ _ ◯ _ _ _
2. _ _ _ _ _ ◯ _
3. _ _ _ ◯ _ _
4. _ _ _ ◯ _ _
5. _ _ _ _ _ _ ◯ _
6. ◯ _ _ _ _ _
7. _ _ _ _ _ ◯
8. ◯ _ _ _ _

Think of yourself with sober
◯◯◯◯◯◯◯.

(Romans 12:3)

Keep Going

1. **CRIDNSEO**
2. **PCATCE**
3. **FGYORIL**
4. **TIMLEAAR**
5. **ATSINS**

6. **RCRUSPITE**
7. **MNERIA**
8. **ASPRIE**
9. **MDCOENN**

1. _ _ ◯ _ _ _ _ _

2. _ ◯ _ _ _ _

3. _ _ _ ◯ _ _ _

4. _ _ _ _ _ _ ◯ _

5. _ _ _ ◯ _ _

6. _ _ _ _ _ _ _ ◯ _ _

7. _ ◯ _ _ _ _

8. _ _ _ _ _ ◯

9. _ _ _ ◯ _ _ _

"May the God who gives

◯◯◯◯◯◯◯ and

encouragement give you a spirit of unity among

yourselves as you follow Christ Jesus."

(Romans 15:5)

Bring On a Hammer

1. IDXEEL
2. HRTOCISI
3. WARSNE
4. SEQRETU
5. DEURLIB
6. DDTECIAE
7. RYLCVAA
8. PERARI

1. ◯ _ _ _ _ _
2. _ _ ◯ _ _ _ _ _
3. _ _ _ _ ◯ _ _
4. _ _ _ ◯ _ _ _
5. _ _ ◯ _ _ _
6. ◯ _ _ _ _ _ _
7. _ _ ◯ _ _ _ _
8. _ _ _ ◯ _

They became ◯◯◯◯◯◯◯◯
to fulfill Nehemiah's vision.

(Nehemiah 2:17–18)

Seeing Ahead

1. **VENATRS**
2. **HNUSTODA**
3. **OEDBRR**
4. **UHDJA**
5. **NHSGIIN**
6. **OEIATBM**
7. **TPONROI**
8. **ORERSPP**

1. _ ◯ _ _ _ _ _
2. _ _ ◯ _ _ _ _ _
3. _ _ _ _ ◯ _
4. _ _ _ ◯ _
5. ◯ _ _ _ _ _ _
6. _ _ _ _ _ ◯ _
7. ◯ _ _ _ _ _ _
8. _ _ _ _ ◯ _ _

"The wife of a man from the company of the
◯◯◯◯◯◯◯ cried out to
Elisha, 'Your servant my husband is dead, and you
know that he revered the LORD. But now his creditor
is coming to take my two boys as his slaves.' "

(2 Kings 4:1)

17

Sons at Work

1. **LPARLI**
2. **UDEGI**
3. **DBAANON**
4. **NJYEO**
5. **HAHISPRD**
6. **EEAXTDL**
7. **DAHLNUF**
8. **OHTTGUH**

1. _ _ _ _ ◯ _
2. _ _ _ _ ◯
3. _ _ _ ◯ _ _ _
4. _ _ ◯ _ _
5. _ _ _ _ ◯ _ _ _
6. _ ◯ _ _ _ _
7. ◯ _ _ _ _ _
8. _ _ _ _ _ ◯ _

"The ◯◯◯◯◯◯◯ Gate was repaired by Joiada son of Paseah and Meshullam son of Besodeiah."

(Nehemiah 3:6)

A Holy Place

1. CLEGTNE
2. MGERRAAI
3. NMHAIHEE
4. KPSAE
5. MOSLNOO

6. RFIEOGN
7. OOSDHHEUL
8. UCCANTO
9. DCAORC
10. NAGRI

1. _ Ⓞ _ _ _ _ _

2. _ _ Ⓞ _ _ _ _

3. _ _ _ Ⓞ _ _ _

4. Ⓞ _ _ _ _

5. _ _ Ⓞ _ _ _ _

6. _ Ⓞ _ _ _ _ _

7. _ _ Ⓞ _ _ _ _ _

8. _ _ _ _ _ Ⓞ

9. _ _ Ⓞ _ _ _

10. _ Ⓞ _ _ _

It was here that Eliashib the priest had been put in charge in the house of God.

(Nehemiah 13:4)

The Road to Jericho

1. IATSNGND
2. NCVENTOA
3. HSOJUA
4. HODTSUNA
5. TEWRA
6. OSESNT
7. CIDRTE
8. LLUFDEFLI
9. AONDJR
10. THONM

1. ◯ _ _ _ _ _ _ _
2. _ _ _ ◯ _ _ _ _
3. _ ◯ _ _ _ _
4. _ _ _ _ ◯ _ _ _
5. _ _ _ ◯ _
6. _ ◯ _ _ _ _
7. _ _ ◯ _ _ _
8. ◯ _ _ ◯ _ _ _ _ _
9. _ ◯ _ _ _
10. _ _ _ _ ◯

" 'Be strong and courageous, because you will lead these people to inherit the land I swore to their ◯◯◯◯◯◯◯◯◯◯ to give them.' "

(Joshua 1:6)

Hungry?

1. HSRICE
2. RPRPTSOIYE
3. NACHSIG
4. ONTIGLI
5. NFBETIE
6. HSRELTE
7. RRSPVEEE
8. RTMEEEX

1. _ _ _ _ Ⓞ _
2. Ⓞ _ _ _ _ _ _ _ _
3. _ _ Ⓞ _ _ _ _
4. _ _ _ _ Ⓞ _ _
5. _ _ _ Ⓞ _ _ _
6. _ _ _ _ Ⓞ _ _
7. Ⓞ _ _ _ _ _ _ _
8. _ _ Ⓞ _ _ _ _

"All man's efforts are for his mouth, yet his

Ⓞ Ⓞ Ⓞ Ⓞ Ⓞ Ⓞ Ⓞ is never

satisfied."

(Ecclesiastes 6:7)

A Safe City

1. ORRTYERIT
2. OHNRT
3. PYCOCU
4. RTOESGNR
5. LPPOEE
6. WOTN
7. SEREDI
8. LGENOB
9. RSEENTA
10. RISELA

1. _ ⃝ _ _ _ _ ⃝ _ _
2. ⃝ _ _ _ _
3. _ _ ⃝ _ _ _
4. _ ⃝ _ _ _ _ _ _
5. _ _ _ _ ⃝ _
6. ⃝ _ _ ⃝ _
7. _ _ _ ⃝ _ _
8. _ _ _ ⃝ _ _
9. _ ⃝ _ _ _ _ ⃝
10. ⃝ _ _ _ _

A place of refuge was provided for those guilty of this.

⃝⃝⃝⃝⃝⃝⃝⃝⃝⃝⃝

killing

(Numbers 35:15)

Yummm. . . !

1. ORDO
2. EOTSNUHR
3. VCRADE
4. DSSTRSIE
5. MSERAST

6. OAHTRIC
7. WIDINWHRL
8. DLCUO
9. VLEEIBE
10. HEOUGN

1. — — — ◯

2. ◯ — — — — — — — —

3. — — ◯ — — —

4. — — — — — ◯ — —

5. — — — ◯ — — —

6. — — ◯ — — —

7. — — — — — — — ◯◯

8. — ◯ — — —

9. ◯ — — — — — —

10. — — — — ◯ —

"Men ate the ◯◯◯◯◯ of ◯◯◯◯◯; he sent them all the food they could eat."

(Psalm 78:25)

God's Wonder

1. TXADLEE
2. CEJOREI
3. RWPOE
4. ORNCENUE
5. NFUDO
6. GRNMOIN
7. YAGNR
8. CEREDU
9. OEHRTN
10. EMNSIEE

1. __ __ __ __ __ __ ⊖__
2. __ __ __ ⊖ __ __ __
3. __ ⊖ __ __ __
4. __ __ __ __ __ ⊖ __ __
5. ⊖ __ __ __ __
6. __ __ __ ⊖ __ __ __
7. ⊖ __ __ __
8. __ __ __ ⊖ __ __
9. ⊖ __ __ __ __ __
10. __ __ __ __ ⊖ __ __

Righteousness and justice are the

⊖ ⊖ ⊖ ⊖ ⊖ ⊖ ⊖ ⊖ ⊖ of God's throne.

(Psalm 89:14)

Just Desert!

1. NBZERO
2. EOHWRSS
3. DTEDNISE
4. CREPROHA
5. FFSEUR
6. OPAPTNI
7. VDRENI
8. UTCHO
9. ITGHF
10. UESRCE

1. — ⊕ — — — — —
2. — — — — — — ⊕
3. — ⊕ — — — — ⊕ —
4. — — — ⊕ — — —
5. ⊕ — — — — —
6. — — ⊕ — — — —
7. — ⊕ — — — —
8. — — ⊕ — — —
9. — — — — ⊕
10. — — — ⊕ — —

"You understand, O LORD; remember me and care for me. Avenge me on my

⊕⊕⊕⊕⊕⊕⊕⊕⊕⊕⊕."

(Jeremiah 15:15)

25

Not That Bright!

1. **OTAIRNNG**
2. **SBACEUE**
3. **ALWMONP**
4. **WRCNO**
5. **PETASLO**
6. **YVELRER**
7. **VAKHINGTNSGI**
8. **TMTDEPE**
9. **IGVNLI**

1. — ⊖ — — — — — — —
2. — — — — — — ⊖
3. — — — ⊖ — — —
4. — — ⊖ — — —
5. — — — — — — ⊖
6. — — — ⊖ — —
7. — — — ⊖ — — — — — —
8. — — — — ⊖
9. — — — — ⊖ —

The man who *thinks* he knows something believes he has this.

⊖ ⊖ ⊖ ⊖ ⊖ ⊖ ⊖ ⊖

(Proverbs 14:7)

Bitter Taste

1. VVROSURI
2. EHSRSPHDE
3. CUPELAEF
4. TWAHR
5. OMEAWDS
6. DURIBE
7. IJCETUS
8. RATDE

1. __ __ __ __ Ⓞ __ __ __

2. __ __ Ⓞ __ __ __ __ __ __

3. __ Ⓞ __ __ __ __ __ __

4. __ __ __ __ Ⓞ

5. Ⓞ __ __ __ __ __ __

6. __ __ Ⓞ __ __ __

7. Ⓞ __ __ __ __ __ __

8. __ __ __ Ⓞ __

To ⓄⓄⓄⓄⓄⓄⓄ, the Lord
spoke that the nations would drink from the cup of
wrath.

(Jeremiah 25:15)

Coming Doom

1. NECHATMR
2. DCEAR
3. ENARBN
4. NOSPEK
5. LOBEHIRR
6. NNEROW
7. SUNHIP
8. ECMLA
9. ESCHRTT
10. EHTILOS

1. _ _ _ _ ⊖ _ _ _
2. _ ⊖ _ _ _
3. _ _ ⊖ _ _
4. _ ⊖ _ _ _ _
5. _ _ _ ⊖ _ _ _
6. _ _ ⊖ _ _ _
7. _ ⊖ _ _ _ _
8. _ ⊖ _ _
9. _ ⊖ _ _ _
10. _ _ ⊖ _ _ _

There was a prophecy of ⊖⊖⊖⊖⊖⊖⊖⊖⊖⊖ against Moab.

(Ezekiel 25:11)

Be Honest

---

1. **MUSBTI**
2. **EROMFR**
3. **UHRCHC**
4. **OERCNNERSTO**
5. **VERSICE**

6. **IETDNU**
7. **DENLSAR**
8. **LOOSHFI**
9. **ELMABLSSE**

1. ◯ _ _ _ _ _
2. _ ◯ _ _ _ _
3. _ _ _ _ ◯
4. _ ◯ _ _ _ _ _ _ _ _ _
5. _ _ _ _ _ _ ◯
6. _ _ _ _ ◯
7. _ ◯ _ _ _ _
8. ◯ _ _ _ _ _ _
9. _ _ ◯ _ _ _ _ _ _

"Therefore each of you must put off
◯◯◯◯◯◯◯◯ and speak
truthfully to his neighbor, for we are all members of
one body."

(Ephesians 4:25)

Not a Bird or a Plane

1. **SGNNTRSSIARSOE**
2. **MARLES**
3. **EISDNKSN**
4. **TRECAE**
5. **AANCVDE**
6. **ULRER**
7. **IODNMONI**
8. **SPEUSHE**

1. _ _ _ _ _ _ -
   _ _ _ _ _ _ _ _ Ⓞ _

2. _ Ⓞ _ _ _ _

3. _ _ Ⓞ _ _ _ _

4. Ⓞ _ _ _ _ _

5. _ _ _ Ⓞ _ _ _ _

6. _ _ Ⓞ _ _

7. Ⓞ _ _ _ _ _ _ _

8. _ _ _ _ _ Ⓞ _

Up, up, and away!

⒪⒪⒪⒪⒪⒪⒪⒪

(Psalm 47:5)

Free at Last

1. DERLE
2. OTCCANU
3. SPUDSRIER
4. DIMLED
5. SESFATDAT
6. AGERDR
7. CPHDEARE
8. EORDEFM

1. _ _ _ (_) _
2. _ _ _ _ (_)(_) _
3. (_) _ _ _ _ _ _ _ _
4. _ (_) _ _ _ _
5. _ _ _ _ _ (_) _ _ _
6. _ _ (_) _ _ _
7. _ (_) _ _ _ _ _ _
8. (_) _ _ _ _ _ _

Done with sin: ◯◯◯◯◯◯◯◯

in the body

(Numbers 14:33)

Made Clean

1. AGAMEIRR
2. ENTUDI
3. VNTECOGI
4. REISDES
5. LVEAS
6. FHTIA
7. MHNAU
8. EUSJS
9. NOBUD
10. LRGNEO
11. RTCHIS
12. NTEALER

1. _ _ _ _ Ⓞ _ _ _
2. _ Ⓞ _ _ _ _
3. _ _ _ Ⓞ _ _ _ _
4. _ _ Ⓞ _ _ _ Ⓞ
5. _ _ _ _ Ⓞ
6. _ _ _ _ Ⓞ
7. Ⓞ _ _ _ _ _
8. _ _ _ Ⓞ _
9. _ Ⓞ _ _ _
10. _ _ _ Ⓞ _ _
11. _ _ _ Ⓞ _
12. _ _ _ Ⓞ _ _ _

We have eternal life in Christ as grace reigns through

Ⓞ Ⓞ Ⓞ Ⓞ Ⓞ Ⓞ Ⓞ Ⓞ Ⓞ Ⓞ Ⓞ Ⓞ.

(Psalm 119:39–41)

A Good Cleansing

1. IUFRPDEI
2. HEDSLI
3. DNNIURGE
4. HEIWRST
5. ROMUN

6. EOBY
7. INSAYCTF
8. MYPTE
9. EISHLMB

1. ○ _ _ _ _ _ _ _
2. _ _ ○ _ _ _
3. _ _ _ ○ _ _ _ _
4. _ _ _ ○ _ _ _
5. _ ○ _ _ _
6. _ _ _ ○
7. _ _ _ ○ _ _ _
8. _ _ _ _ ○
9. _ _ _ _ ○ _

"Therefore, rid yourselves of all malice and all deceit, ○○○○○○○○○, envy, and slander of every kind."

(1 Peter 2:1)

33

The Truth

1. **ETNCORAS**
2. **PTALIMRAI**
3. **MBSIUT**
4. **EHMULB**
5. **BHRROA**
6. **LFESSIH**
7. **ENRECSI**
8. **NVTCICO**

1. ◯ _ _ _ _ _ _ _

2. _ _ _ _ _ _ ◯ _ _

3. _ _ ◯ _ _ _

4. _ _ ◯ _ _ _

5. _ _ _ _ ◯ _

6. _ _ _ _ ◯ _ _

7. _ _ ◯ _ _ _ _

8. _ _ _ _ _ _ ◯

"But if you harbor bitter envy and selfish ◯◯◯◯◯◯◯ in your hearts, do not boast about it or deny the truth."

(James 3:14)

34

A Good Reflection

1. **UERDHDS**
2. **MRIORR**
3. **OUPTRCR**
4. **MATE**
5. **ARYLO**
6. **OXEPLIT**
7. **DAFNIG**

1. _ _ _ _ Ⓞ _ _
2. Ⓞ _ _ _ _ _
3. _ _ _ Ⓞ _ _ _
4. _ _ _ Ⓞ
5. _ Ⓞ _ _ _
6. Ⓞ _ _ _ _ _ _
7. Ⓞ _ _ _ _ _

Look into the perfect law and receive

Ⓞ Ⓞ Ⓞ Ⓞ Ⓞ Ⓞ Ⓞ .

(James 1:25)

35

A Holy Vision

1. DIODHCHLO
2. IITECERTAFC
3. LVPOENEE
4. THOGERTE
5. UARGE

6. TBYEARED
7. WLFALU
8. EKBURE
9. NODLGIESS
10. ITGASAN

1. __ __ Ⓞ __ __ __ __ __ __
2. __ __ __ __ __ __ __ __ Ⓞ __
3. __ Ⓞ __ __ __ __ __ __
4. __ __ __ __ __ Ⓞ __
5. __ __ __ __ Ⓞ
6. __ __ __ Ⓞ Ⓞ __ __ __
7. __ __ __ Ⓞ __ __
8. __ __ __ Ⓞ __
9. Ⓞ __ __ __ __ __ __ __ __
10. __ __ __ __ __ Ⓞ __

To make as white as the light.

Ⓞ Ⓞ Ⓞ Ⓞ Ⓞ Ⓞ Ⓞ Ⓞ Ⓞ Ⓞ

(Matthew 17:2)

Close to the End

1. **INSNTAO**
2. **MDNDCEONE**
3. **YHRUTOATI**
4. **GGLSNUAEA**
5. **OCNVLEEI**
6. **SBEDLSE**
7. **OEBR**

Smoke will rise high from this place.

(Isaiah 21:9)

Be Very Careful

1. **KTRISE**
2. **IDLEVRE**
3. **OBRSTED**
4. **UESEMAR**
5. **RRWYO**
6. **WOBRRO**
7. **OEGIVFR**
8. **CSEPIE**
9. **NDRUE**

1. _ _ _ _ _ Ⓞ
2. _ _ _ Ⓞ _ _ _
3. _ _ _ _ Ⓞ _ _
4. _ _ _ Ⓞ _ _ _
5. _ Ⓞ _ _ _ _
6. _ _ _ Ⓞ _ _
7. Ⓞ _ _ _ _ _ _
8. _ _ _ Ⓞ _ _
9. Ⓞ _ _ _ _

" 'Watch out for false prophets. They come to you in sheep's clothing, but inwardly they are

Ⓞ Ⓞ Ⓞ Ⓞ Ⓞ Ⓞ Ⓞ Ⓞ Ⓞ wolves.' "

(Matthew 7:15)

God Help Me!

1. **OWRORS**
2. **NAGMEII**
3. **OUDBN**
4. **EWTINSS**
5. **RNLGEI**
6. **URAKRNDD**
7. **OYLFL**

1. _ _ _ _ _ ◯
2. _ _ ◯ _ _ _ _
3. _ _ _ _ ◯
4. ◯ _ _ _ _ _ _
5. _ _ _ _ _ ◯
6. _ _ _ _ _ ◯ _ _
7. _ _ _ _ ◯

A narrow well is this wife.

◯◯◯◯◯◯◯

(Proverbs 23:27)

Wrong Kind of Love

1. ECWKID
2. EWART
3. FLRCETE
4. EVSRLI
5. CMELIA

6. DDNUSE
7. ITHNNGO
8. EDGYRE
9. PENARSH
10. NEISNEC

1. ◯ _ _ _ _ _
2. _ _ _ ◯ _
3. _ ◯ _ ◯ _ _ _
4. _ _ _ ◯ _ _
5. ◯ _ _ _ _ _
6. _ _ _ _ ◯ _
7. _ ◯ _ _ _ _ ◯
8. _ ◯ _ _ _
9. _ ◯ _ _ _ _ _
10. ◯ _ _ _ _ _ _

"Anger is cruel and fury

◯◯◯◯◯◯◯◯◯◯◯,

but who can stand before jealousy?"

(Proverbs 27:4)

40

Sharp Words

1. **NRNMOGI**
2. **NNMASLEEISG**
3. **GDNARE**
4. **MRBRMEEE**
5. **HEDNDI**
6. **LSBDESE**
7. **WFATDERAR**
8. **NMSSDEA**

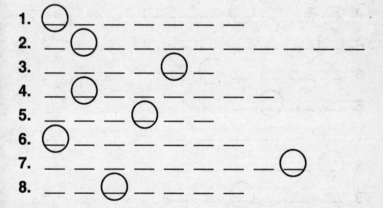

1. ◯ __ __ __ __ __ __
2. __ ◯ __ __ __ __ __ __ __ __
3. __ __ ◯ __
4. __ ◯ __ __ __ __ __
5. __ __ __ ◯ __ __
6. ◯ __ __ __ __ __
7. __ __ __ __ __ __ ◯ __
8. __ __ ◯ __ __ __ __

"The words of the wise are like goads, their collected sayings like firmly ◯◯◯◯◯◯◯◯ nails—given by one Shepherd."

(Ecclesiastes 12:11)

A Change of God's Mind

1. IDLEEF
2. MSNCUEO
3. SPRPESO
4. MBNREU
5. WESOR

6. ENSRA
7. DRETCI
8. OCMSSTU
9. NFMAEI
10. NASHD

1. _ _ _ ◯ _ ◯
2. _ _ ◯ _ _ _ _
3. _ _ _ ◯ _ _ _
4. ◯ _ _ _ _ _
5. _ _ _ _ ◯
6. _ _ ◯ _ _ _
7. _ _ _ _ _ ◯
8. ◯ _ _ _ _ _ _
9. _ _ _ ◯ _ _
10. ◯ _ _ _ _

"Therefore the LORD was angry with his people and abhorred his

◯ ◯ ◯ ◯ ◯ ◯ ◯ ◯ ◯ ◯."

(Psalm 106:40)

Into Thin Air?

1. TPECNDEIO
2. OCETPTR
3. KIWEDC
4. IVNA
5. FCRNUAE
6. TSCIEJU
7. NSNITOA
8. ERTHA

1. ◯ __ __ __ __ __ __ __ __
2. __ __ __ __ ◯ __ __
3. __ ◯ __ __ __ __
4. ◯ __ __ __
5. __ __ __ ◯ __ __ __
6. __ __ ◯ __ __ __
7. __ ◯ __ __ __ __ __
8. ◯ __ __ __ __

Where are the godly? The faithful have

◯◯◯◯◯◯◯◯.

(Psalm 12:1)

Stand Strong

1. MWNAO
2. OYALNBB
3. AAPBTTRLESE
4. ELPTEM
5. NMKNDIA

6. LRATA
7. CSMOHAT
8. RDYSTEO
9. TRRTONE

1. — — ◯ — —
2. — — — ◯ — — —
3. — — — — — — — — — — ◯
4. ◯ — — — — — —
5. — — — ◯ — — —
6. — — ◯ — — —
7. — — ◯ — — — —
8. — — ◯ — — —
9. — — — — ◯ — —

"Now when they have finished their ◯◯◯◯ ◯◯◯ ◯, the beast that comes up from the Abyss will attack them, and overpower and kill them."

(Revelation 11:7)

44

Yuck!

1. ACRTNUI
2. MCRYEEON
3. NENCULA
4. GVENNIE
5. EBRDUN
6. NFOFGRIE
7. HBTAE
8. ODLOB

1. — — — — — — ◯
2. — — ◯ — — ◯ — —
3. — — — — ◯ — — —
4. — — — — ◯ — — —
5. — — — — — ◯
6. — ◯ — — — — — — —
7. ◯ — — — —
8. — — — — ◯

◯ ◯ ◯ ◯ ◯ ◯ ◯ ◯

Don't eat this!

◯ ◯ ◯ ◯ ◯ ◯ ◯ ◯ ◯ blood

(Leviticus 7:21–23, 26–27)

45

Clean as a Whistle

1. ASENTECCOR
2. CEPACT
3. CFEETD
4. AELUV
5. RRMGEAIA
6. YITHLF
7. LOAWL
8. FNEROAP
9. RDOL
10. UHTOC

1. __ __ __ Ⓞ __ __ __ __ __ __
2. __ __ __ __ Ⓞ __
3. __ Ⓞ __ __ __ __
4. __ __ Ⓞ __ __ __
5. __ __ __ __ Ⓞ __ __ __ __
6. Ⓞ __ __ __ __ __
7. __ __ __ __ Ⓞ
8. __ __ Ⓞ __ __ __ __
9. Ⓞ __ __ __
10. __ __ __ __ Ⓞ

"When anyone brings from the herd or flock a
Ⓞ Ⓞ Ⓞ Ⓞ Ⓞ Ⓞ Ⓞ Ⓞ offering
to the LORD to fulfill a special vow or as a freewill
offering, it must be without defect or blemish to be
acceptable."

(Leviticus 22:21)

A Job for Everyone

1. OWANM
2. FECNOSS
3. TONREIDCI
4. CRASDE
5. ECENTRAN

6. CSRTLEAI
7. RTVELAIE
8. LGDO
9. VEESR
10. NTTHE

1. _ _ _ _ ⬭
2. _ ⬭ _ _ _ _
3. _ _ ⬭ _ _ _ _ _ _
4. ⬭ _ _ _ _ _
5. _ _ _ _ _ _ _ ⬭
6. _ _ ⬭ _ _ _ ⬭ _
7. _ _ _ _ ⬭ _ _
8. ⬭ _ _ _
9. ⬭ _ _ _ _
10. _ _ _ _ ⬭

These clans carried the curtains for the tabernacle, the tent of meeting.

(Numbers 3:25)

Slither!

1. SCKVTOIEL
2. OENZBR
3. YJRNEUO
4. RVLTAE
5. SGREESMNE
6. DTRYOES
7. LAVTEIO
8. DDNIEE

1. _ _ _ _ ⊖ _ _ _ _
2. _ _ ⊖ _ _ _
3. _ _ ⊖ _ _ _
4. _ _ _ _ ⊖ _ _
5. ⊖ _ _ _ _ _ _ _ _
6. _ _ _ _ _ ⊖ _
7. ⊖ _ _ _ _ _
8. _ _ ⊖ _ _ _

When the Israelites spoke against the Lord and
Moses, ⊖⊖⊖⊖⊖⊖⊖⊖ snakes
were sent among them.

(Numbers 21:5–6)

A New Job

1. LISITHEIPN
2. CSDIGREA
3. RANTESV
4. VADDI
5. ERLIVDE
6. ULAMSE
7. NCTUI

1. — — — — — — — ◯ — —
2. — — — — ◯ — — —
3. ◯ — — — — — —
4. — — ◯ — —
5. — — — — — ◯ —
6. — — — — ◯ —
7. — — — — ◯

"David came to Saul and entered his
◯◯◯◯◯◯◯. Saul liked him
very much, and David became one of his
armor-bearers."

(1 Samuel 16:21)

49

My Very Own City!

1. **EROBHN**
2. **BTESIJEU**
3. **NNAITO**
4. **ETFAS**
5. **WLELASS**
6. **FSINGFORP**
7. **EOHUS**
8. **MROSEPI**

1. __ __ __ Ⓞ __ __

2. __ Ⓞ __ __ __ __ __ __

3. __ __ __ __ __ Ⓞ

4. Ⓞ __ __ __ __ __

5. __ __ __ __ __ __ Ⓞ

6. __ __ __ __ __ Ⓞ __ __ __

7. __ Ⓞ __ __ __

8. __ __ __ __ __ Ⓞ __

David captured the

Ⓞ Ⓞ Ⓞ Ⓞ Ⓞ Ⓞ Ⓞ of Zion and would

call it the City of David.

(2 Samuel 5:7)

To Know. . .or Not to Know

1. **HLTIYUMI**
2. **CENMAPDCAOI**
3. **RNVPGEEAI**
4. **RCDEPOU**
5. **RNISPG**
6. **WSLTHSERO**

1. _ _ Ⓞ _ _ _ _ _
2. _ _ Ⓞ _ _ _ _ _ _
3. _ _ _ _ _ _ Ⓞ _ _
4. _ _ _ Ⓞ _ _ _
5. Ⓞ _ _ _ _ _
6. Ⓞ _ _ _ _ _ _

Two sides of true Ⓞ Ⓞ Ⓞ Ⓞ Ⓞ Ⓞ

(Job 11:6)

Who Could It Be?

1. **ESUFRE**
2. **GRISACED**
3. **TEITHTI**
4. **IHCEBTRLAP**
5. **NOTEDAIN**
6. **TOLSILNEM**
7. **NGRODU**
8. **WRARO**
9. **LAESDTEO**

1. — — — Ⓞ — —
2. — — — — — — Ⓞ —
3. Ⓞ — — — — — —
4. — — — — Ⓞ — — — — — —
5. — — — — — — Ⓞ —
6. — — — Ⓞ — — — — —
7. — — Ⓞ — — —
8. — — — Ⓞ —
9. — — Ⓞ — — — — —

"This is what the LORD says: 'Out of your own
Ⓞ Ⓞ Ⓞ Ⓞ Ⓞ Ⓞ Ⓞ Ⓞ I am going to
bring calamity upon you.' "

(2 Samuel 12:11)

52

A Roving Eye

1. LFTWEHT   5. ESEDAPL
2. MANAH   6. EONBL
3. IOGDMKN   7. FICOFRE
4. MUONMS   8. RDGUAED

1. _ _ _ _ _ ⊖ _
2. _ ⊖ _ _ _
3. _ ⊖ _ _ _ _ _
4. _ ⊖ _ _ _ _
5. _ ⊖ _ _ _ ⊖ _
6. _ _ ⊖ _ _
7. _ ⊖ _ _ _ _ _
8. _ ⊖ _ _ _ _ _

King Xerxes was looking for a

⊖⊖⊖⊖⊖⊖⊖⊖ young wife.

(Esther 2:1–2)

53

What a Party!

1. RIAPES
2. AELFREW
3. EPLEOP
4. CANTCOU
5. EBTTER
6. TINONCEU
7. MORCAEDI
8. ALYMIF
9. EFRLIE
10. URIOERC

1. _ _ _ _ _ Ⓞ
2. _ Ⓞ _ _ _ _ _
3. _ _ _ _ Ⓞ
4. _ Ⓞ _ _ _ _ _
5. Ⓞ _ _ Ⓞ _ _
6. _ _ _ _ Ⓞ _ _
7. _ _ Ⓞ _ _ _ _
8. _ _ _ _ Ⓞ
9. _ _ _ Ⓞ _ _
10. _ Ⓞ _ _ _ _ _

"So the Jews agreed to continue the Ⓞ Ⓞ Ⓞ Ⓞ Ⓞ Ⓞ Ⓞ Ⓞ Ⓞ Ⓞ they had begun, doing what Mordecai had written to them."

(Esther 9:23)

Be Fair to God

---

1. NRSOWDE
2. IAELMRC
3. PWRDAU
4. OTALMR
5. HSHPRDIA

6. RLIOTUM
7. GHNTI
8. TEGTYNRII
9. LDEDIG
10. OUNTC

1. Ⓞ _ _ _ _ _ _

2. _ _ Ⓞ _ _ _ _

3. _ _ _ _ Ⓞ _

4. _ Ⓞ _ _ _ _

5. _ _ _ _ _ _ Ⓞ _

6. _ _ _ _ Ⓞ _ _

7. Ⓞ _ _ _ _

8. _ _ Ⓞ _ _ _ _ _

9. Ⓞ _ _ _ _ _

10. _ _ _ Ⓞ _

"In all this, Job did not sin by charging God with
Ⓞ Ⓞ Ⓞ Ⓞ Ⓞ Ⓞ Ⓞ Ⓞ Ⓞ."

(Job 1:22)

55

Going Home

1. **ENPRCETAEN**
2. **NAREG**
3. **PCAEE**
4. **SMGSEEA**
5. **VWHRRTOOE**
6. **MJEBNINA**
7. **ROESMIP**
8. **BTHABSA**

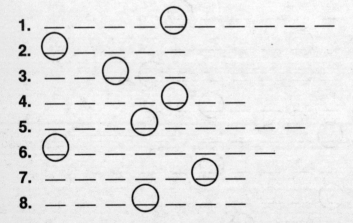

1. — — — — ◯ — — — — —
2. ◯ — — — —
3. — ◯ — — —
4. — — ◯ — —
5. — — ◯ — — — —
6. ◯ — — — — — —
7. — — — ◯ — —
8. — — — ◯ — — —

"When ◯◯◯◯◯◯◯ and Saul had finished their mission, they returned from Jerusalem, taking with them John, also called Mark."

(Acts 12:25)

What Great Love

1. **RMILGAEPIG**
2. **AIHTYMLG**
3. **TRTHEGSN**
4. **VFARO**
5. **CRINEP**
6. **UUDESB**
7. **EOWTSB**
8. **RSTTU**

1. _ Ⓞ _ _ _ _ _ _ Ⓞ _
2. Ⓞ _ _ _ _ _ _ _
3. _ _ _ _ Ⓞ _ _ _
4. _ _ _ Ⓞ _
5. _ _ _ Ⓞ _ _
6. _ _ _ Ⓞ _ _
7. Ⓞ _ _ _ _ _
8. _ _ Ⓞ _ _ _

"You are forgiving and good, O Lord,

Ⓞ Ⓞ Ⓞ Ⓞ Ⓞ Ⓞ Ⓞ Ⓞ in love to all

who call to you."

(Psalm 86:5)

A Godly Memory

1. ETORRDIC
2. MNREAI
3. GIHH
4. SPHIREW
5. MMRYOE
6. UGRNHY
7. ILYQETU
8. DERONUFWL

1. __ __ __ __ __ Ⓞ __ __

2. __ __ __ __ Ⓞ __

3. __ Ⓞ __ __

4. __ __ Ⓞ __ __ __ __

5. __ __ __ __ Ⓞ

6. __ Ⓞ __ __ __ __

7. Ⓞ __ __ __ __ __ __

8. __ __ Ⓞ __ __ __ __ __ __

Of an evil man, may his

◯◯◯◯◯◯◯ be

remembered before the Lord.

(Psalm 109:14)

Light of the Word

1. **IINGLLW**
2. **OTTEPSSFO**
3. **DREMEE**
4. **AUSTTET**
5. **SUNHIP**
6. **SIDONCER**
7. **HELSDI**
8. **RESONOPSIP**

1. _ _ _ _ _ _ ◯
2. ◯ _ _ _ _ _ _ _ _
3. _ _ ◯ _ _ _
4. _ _ _ ◯ _ _
5. _ _ ◯ _ _
6. _ ◯ _ _ _ _
7. _ _ ◯ _ ◯ _
8. _ _ _ _ _ _ _ _ _ ◯

"The ◯◯◯◯◯◯◯◯ of your words gives light; it gives understanding to the simple."

(Psalm 119:130)

I See!

1. CPTSEEPR
2. OPUDR
3. CKWEDI
4. AWERNS
5. RSCUOE
6. NNSHDUE
7. RUDCEPEN
8. ANTBUNDA
9. THUMO
10. IPRUHGT

1. _ ◯ _ _ _ _ _ _
2. _ _ ◯ _ _
3. _ _ _ _ ◯ _
4. _ _ _ _ _ ◯
5. ◯ _ _ _ _ _
6. _ _ _ _ ◯ _ _
7. _ _ _ _ _ ◯ _
8. _ _ _ _ _ _ ◯
9. _ ◯ _ _ _
10. _ _ ◯ _ _ _

Heed this and you will have understanding.

◯◯◯◯◯◯◯◯◯◯

(Proverbs 15:32)

60

Better to Be Hated

1. CEONNCR
2. OWRTHG
3. SJICETU
4. CELONCA
5. IOSWMD
6. OTBAS
7. MELSSLEBA
8. RSPROPE
9. ADFE
10. RERYAP

1. — O — — — O —
2. — — — — — O
3. — — — O — — —
4. — O — — — — —
5. — O — — — —
6. — — — — O
7. O — — — — — O — — —
8. — — — O — — —
9. O — — —
10. — — — O — —

"OOOOOOOOOOO
men hate a man of integrity and seek to kill the
upright."

(Proverbs 29:10)

61

What a Name!

1. **MERNUB**
2. **IOVSIN**
3. **TMYERL**
4. **EASHK**
5. **ERISDA**
6. **SURMEAE**
7. **PECASE**
8. **ZAPTIEB**
9. **HUTSO**

1. — — — — Ⓞ —

2. — Ⓞ — — — —

3. — — Ⓞ — — —

4. — Ⓞ — — —

5. — Ⓞ — — — —

6. — — Ⓞ — — — —

7. — — Ⓞ — — —

8. — — — — — Ⓞ —

9. — Ⓞ — — —

Ⓞ Ⓞ Ⓞ Ⓞ Ⓞ Ⓞ Ⓞ Ⓞ Ⓞ Ⓞ Ⓞ Ⓞ Ⓞ

This king's name is hard to spell.

Ⓞ Ⓞ Ⓞ Ⓞ Ⓞ Ⓞ Ⓞ Ⓞ

(2 Kings 14:29)

Never Changing

1. FREADDUL
2. EERSRPVE
3. AEPRS
4. EREDECS
5. RSPEROP
6. NEAHLIG
7. GWNIS
8. ALTRMEP
9. RHSHA
10. OGHUEN

1. ◯ _ _ _ ◯ _ _ _
2. _ _ _ _ ◯ _ _ _
3. ◯ _ _ _ _
4. _ _ ◯ _ _ _ _
5. _ _ _ ◯ _ _ _
6. _ ◯ _ _ _ _ _
7. _ _ ◯ _ _
8. ◯ _ _ _ _ _ _
9. _ ◯ _ _ _
10. _ ◯ _ _ _ _

" 'I the LORD do not change. So you, O

◯◯◯◯◯◯◯◯◯ of

Jacob, are not destroyed.' "

(Malachi 3:6)

Laban's Heartache

1. **AANLB**
2. **STGHNTRE**
3. **THFREA**
4. **HRLECA**
5. **MANSILA**
6. **RHUSTOG**

7. **TCDEIE**
8. **SNVEE**
9. **NHRTIEI**
10. **LADGEI**
11. **RBHSNAEC**

1. — ⭕ — — —
2. — ⭕ — — — —
3. — — — ⭕ — —
4. ⭕ — — — — —
5. — ⭕ — — ⭕ —
6. — — — ⭕ — —
7. ⭕ — — — — —
8. — — — ⭕ — —
9. ⭕ — ⭕ — — — —
10. — — — — ⭕ —
11. — — — — ⭕ — — — —

Laban kissed his
◯◯◯◯◯◯◯◯◯◯◯◯◯
and daughters good-bye.

(Genesis 31:55)

A Fair Hearing

1. **ARVOF**
2. **LTEFFDAIC**
3. **KVEDEOR**
4. **OEHMENRS**
5. **STREPAU**
6. **GHSLATERU**

1. _ _ _ _ ◯

2. _ _ _ _ _ _ _ ◯

3. ◯ _ _ _ _ _ _

4. _ _ _ _ _ _ ◯ _

5. _ _ _ _ _ ◯

6. _ _ _ _ _ _ ◯ _

" 'These are the things you are to do: Speak the truth to each other, and ◯◯◯◯◯◯ true and sound judgment in your courts.' "

(Zechariah 8:16)

A Good Ol' Boy

1. **OYBLOD**
2. **NNGBUIR**
3. **ODSEDLOHB**
4. **TERATELO**
5. **OEKNWDGLE**
6. **ODORKWOW**
7. **RINDAO**
8. **DKRDANRU**

1. ◯ __ __ __ __ __
2. __ ◯ __ __ __ __ __
3. __ __ __ __ __ ◯ __ __
4. __ __ __ ◯ __ __
5. ◯ __ __ __ __ __ __ __ __
6. __ __ __ __ __ __ ◯
7. __ __ ◯ __ __
8. __ __ __ ◯ __ __ __ __

Another hard name to spell.

◯◯◯◯◯◯◯◯

Too Much to Lose

1. OSNETS
2. AOBLR
3. AEUSTHX
4. ENCRAISE
5. MINTPLAOC
6. HRYEACTRE
7. COFSF
8. SOCULTS
9. RTFOESRS
10. IFG

1. _ _ _ ○ _ _

2. _ _ _ ○

3. _ _ _ _ _ ○

4. ○ _ _ _ _ _ _

5. _ _ _ _ _ ○ _ _

6. _ ○ _ _ _ _ _ _

7. _ _ _ ○

8. _ ○ _ _ _ _

9. ○ _ _ _ _ _ _

10. _ _ ○

"You have plotted the ruin of many peoples,
shaming your own house and
○○○○○○○○○ your life."

(Habbakuk 2:10)

67

Do You Remember Me?

1. OSBNE
2. TROCTEP
3. VTOINALAS
4. NCAEVIITD
5. LWEDL

6. ERCPIED
7. ULDHOP
8. AINSTSU
9. CRUNTOE

1. _ ◯ _ _ _

2. ◯ _ _ _ _ _ _

3. ◯ _ _ _ _ _ _ _ _

4. _ _ _ _ _ _ _ ◯

5. _ _ ◯ _ _

6. ◯ _ _ _ _ _

7. _ _ _ _ _ ◯

8. _ _ ◯ _ _ _ _

9. ◯ _ _ _ _ _ _

"I say to God my Rock, 'Why have you forgotten me? Why must I go about mourning,

◯◯◯◯◯◯◯◯ by the enemy?' "

(Psalm 42:9)

68

What a Word!

1. GGLAGIN
2. EOSSPSS
3. ISRPAE
4. CITQUA
5. RATTE
6. LARAT
7. MANOMDC
8. STETDE
9. USOL
10. RARMY

1. __ __ __ __ __ Ⓞ __
2. __ Ⓞ __ __ __ __ __
3. __ __ __ __ Ⓞ __
4. __ __ __ Ⓞ __ __ __
5. __ __ __ Ⓞ __
6. __ __ __ __ Ⓞ
7. __ __ Ⓞ __ __ __ Ⓞ
8. __ Ⓞ __ __ __ __
9. __ Ⓞ __ __
10. __ __ __ __ Ⓞ

Old Testament book of the Bible.

Ⓞ Ⓞ Ⓞ Ⓞ Ⓞ Ⓞ Ⓞ Ⓞ Ⓞ Ⓞ Ⓞ

So Generous!

1. AERITSMO
2. NWALEER
3. RFSAKOE
4. TTCRA
5. EPORTR

6. URNTB
7. REUBID
8. EAERDSIBL
9. MITYHILU
10. OURYCTN

1. _ _ _ ◯ _ _ _ _
2. _ ◯ _ _ _ _ _
3. _ _ _ _ ◯ _ _
4. _ _ _ ◯ _
5. _ ◯ _ _ _ _ ◯ _
6. _ _ _ ◯ _ _
7. _ _ _ ◯ _ _ _
8. _ _ _ ◯ _ _ _ _ _
9. ◯ _ _ _ _ _ _ _
10. _ _ _ ◯ _ _ _

"Then Joshua sent the people away, each to his own ◯◯◯◯◯◯◯◯◯◯◯."

(Joshua 24:28)

A Choice

1. **ETHAD**
2. **MSLFEHI**
3. **LAVEE**
4. **RTFOUNE**
5. **WERTO**
6. **EANIGRD**
7. **RAGOUCE**
8. **FRIDAA**
9. **EATHRG**
10. **ACAIS**

1. — — — Ⓞ —
2. — Ⓞ — — — — —
3. — — — — Ⓞ
4. — Ⓞ — — Ⓞ — —
5. — Ⓞ — — —
6. — — — — Ⓞ —
7. Ⓞ — — — — — —
8. — — — — Ⓞ
9. — — Ⓞ — — —
10. — Ⓞ — — —

"See, I set before you today life and prosperity, death and

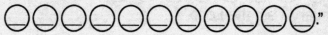."

Godly Respect

1. **ERLDLEY**
2. **GTHELN**
3. **CEVEDEI**
4. **OHSTNE**
5. **UIANTEQTIS**

6. **ANDRDSTA**
7. **GVFREIO**
8. **VINDEI**
9. **ATCS**

1. _ _ _ _ Ⓞ _ _
2. _ Ⓞ _ _ _ _
3. _ _ _ _ _ _ Ⓞ
4. _ _ Ⓞ _ _ _ _
5. _ _ _ _ _ _ _ _ Ⓞ _
6. _ _ _ _ _ Ⓞ _
7. _ _ _ _ Ⓞ _
8. _ _ _ _ Ⓞ
9. Ⓞ _ _ _

" 'Observe my Sabbaths and have

Ⓞ Ⓞ Ⓞ Ⓞ Ⓞ Ⓞ Ⓞ Ⓞ   for my

sanctuary. I am the LORD.' "

(Leviticus 19:30)

A New Life

1. **BAKEHER**
2. **EBULHTE**
3. **ATMRSE**
4. **SSCCUES**
5. **LCMASE**
6. **TRLEBCSEA**
7. **SLEIAMH**

1. _ _ _ _ Ⓞ _ _
2. _ _ _ _ Ⓞ _
3. _ _ _ Ⓞ _ _
4. _ _ _ Ⓞ _ _
5. _ Ⓞ _ _ _
6. Ⓞ _ _ _ _ _ _
7. _ _ Ⓞ _ _ _ _

Another wife for Abraham.
Ⓞ Ⓞ Ⓞ Ⓞ Ⓞ Ⓞ Ⓞ

(Genesis 25:1)

73

Be Faithful

1. **TRUFI**
2. **EECTSRP**
3. **LINSEA**
4. **PRACHAPO**
5. **NORDISHO**

6. **AOOTTT**
7. **MUREIP**
8. **ETNGMEI**
9. **LTUGI**
10. **NEYVIRAD**

1. __ Ⓞ __ __ __
2. __ __ Ⓞ __ __ __ __
3. __ __ __ __ __ Ⓞ
4. __ Ⓞ __ __ __ __ __ __
5. __ __ Ⓞ __ __ __ __
6. __ __ __ Ⓞ __ __
7. Ⓞ __ __ __ __ __
8. __ __ __ Ⓞ __ __ __
9. __ __ Ⓞ __ __
10. __ Ⓞ __ __ __ __ __ __

" 'Do not turn to mediums or seek out

Ⓞ Ⓞ Ⓞ Ⓞ Ⓞ Ⓞ Ⓞ Ⓞ Ⓞ, for you

will be defiled by them. I am the Lord your God.' "

(Leviticus 19:31)

A Time of Humility

1. **NECTFI**
2. **VNTHSEE**
3. **WELLNGSI**
4. **AEHDVS**
5. **RONUNCEOP**
6. **MAXENIE**
7. **THLOESC**
8. **SMTYU**

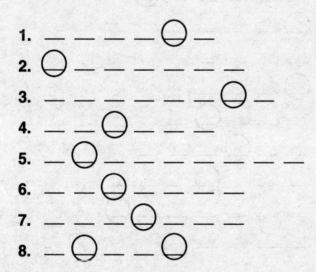

1. _ _ _ _ ◯ _
2. ◯ _ _ _ _ _ _
3. _ _ _ _ _ ◯ _
4. _ _ ◯ _ _ _
5. _ ◯ _ _ _ _ _ _ _
6. _ ◯ _ _ _ _
7. _ _ _ ◯ _ _ _
8. _ ◯ _ _ ◯

A place of worship.

◯◯◯◯◯◯◯◯◯

A Godly Diet

1. FSHEL
2. ISASEDE
3. LOWELY
4. BINGE
5. FDEAD

6. ITPRES
7. SOLTEIA
8. CATUREER
9. ANTRENGP
10. DYLAE

1. _ _ ◯ _ _
2. _ _ _ _ _ _ ◯
3. _ ◯ _ _ _ _
4. ◯ _ _ _ _
5. _ ◯ _ _ _
6. _ _ _ _ ◯ _
7. _ _ _ ◯ _ _ _
8. _ _ _ _ ◯ _ _ _
9. _ _ _ _ _ _ _ ◯
10. ◯ _ _ _ _

" 'Every creature that moves about on the ground is ◯◯◯◯◯◯◯◯◯; it is not to be eaten.' "

(Leviticus 11:41)

76

Camping Trip?

1. **ACOJB**
2. **UAREFCL**
3. **DVINTIOAIN**
4. **LDREHINC**
5. **DENSAMI**
6. **KLEECDSP**
7. **OUTHRG**

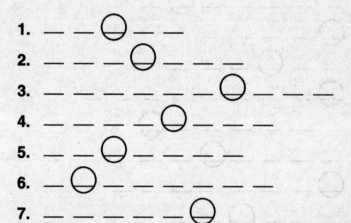

Set up a tent.

Packing Up

1. ICOTNED
2. BANAL
3. LCKFOS
4. USEOLHOHD
5. LSEDSBE
6. SANVTER
7. DRAMAKEN
8. RCHANB

1. _ _ _ _ _ ⊖ _
2. ⊖ _ _ _ _
3. _ _ ⊖ _ _ _
4. ⊖ _ _ _ _ _ _ _ _
5. _ _ _ _ _ ⊖ _
6. _ _ _ _ ⊖ _ _
7. ⊖ _ _ _ _ _ _
8. _ _ ⊖ _ _

"After Rachel gave birth to Joseph, Jacob said to Laban, 'Send me on my way so I can go back to my own ⊖⊖⊖⊖⊖⊖⊖.' "

(Genesis 30:25)

The Hard Way

1. **RADBE**
2. **ADEEDEND**
3. **TFAHI**
4. **MPAXLEE**
5. **LFWOOL**
6. **GYRIFOL**
7. **UQCKLYI**

1. _ _ _ ◯ _
2. _ _ _ _ ◯ _ _
3. _ _ ◯ _ _
4. _ _ _ _ ◯ _
5. _ _ _ _ ◯
6. ◯ _ _ _ _ _ _
7. _ _ _ _ ◯ _ _

A method of travel.

Too Many Voices

1. FFTULRIU
2. CSLNA
3. VOENNTAC
4. TREMAGN
5. RETURCEA
6. LDOOF
7. NFRESOGFI
8. SBESHITAL
9. SOYGNTEU

1. __ __ Ⓞ __ __ __ __ __
2. __ __ __ Ⓞ __
3. __ __ __ __ Ⓞ __ __
4. Ⓞ __ __ __ __ __ __
5. __ __ Ⓞ __ __ __ __
6. __ Ⓞ __ __ __
7. __ __ __ __ __ __ Ⓞ __
8. __ Ⓞ __ __ __ __ __ __
9. __ __ __ Ⓞ __ __ __

It was hard to get any work done with men speaking so many different Ⓞ Ⓞ Ⓞ Ⓞ Ⓞ Ⓞ Ⓞ Ⓞ .

(Genesis 11:6–7)

Big Cheese

1. **FSREUE**
2. **VISDDAE**
3. **AERGHC**
4. **UFYCRCI**
5. **NIISTNGEL**
6. **METEPL**
7. **CURREIPTS**
8. **AIFYSTS**

1. Ⓞ — — — — —
2. — — — — — Ⓞ —
3. — Ⓞ — — — —
4. — — — — Ⓞ — —
5. — — Ⓞ — — — — — —
6. — — — — — Ⓞ
7. — — — — Ⓞ — — — —
8. — Ⓞ — — — —

One of prominent position.

Salvation

1. MPTRUET
2. DEDOUSN
3. UBERNM
4. RIBET
5. GANICGIT
6. OPNIOCRS
7. HOEREADF
8. EPWOR
9. EMKOS
10. TRKEIS

1. _ O _ _ _ _ _
2. _ _ O _ _ _ _
3. O _ _ _ O _
4. _ O _ _ _
5. _ _ _ _ O _ _
6. _ O _ _ _ _ _
7. _ O _ _ _ O _ _
8. _ _ _ O _
9. O _ _ _ _
10. _ _ _ O _ _

Jesus said, "I am the

O O O O O O O O O O

and the life."

(John 11:25)

Coming Dread

1. BYNBALO
2. LONEMLSTI
3. OUMENSC
4. RDBIE
5. DIRER
6. TUDMUTLIE
7. AEOSTLP
8. ORTUETR
9. AERRIACG
10. BLDOEU

1. _ _ _ _ _ _ ◯
2. _ _ _ _ ◯ _ _ _ _
3. _ _ _ _ _ ◯ _
4. _ _ ◯ _
5. _ ◯ _ _ _
6. _ ◯ _ _ _ _ _
7. _ ◯ _ _ _ _
8. ◯ _ _ _ _ _
9. _ _ _ _ ◯ _ _
10. _ ◯ _ _ _ _

" 'When you see Jerusalem being surrounded by armies, you will know that its

◯◯◯◯◯◯◯◯◯◯ is near.' "

(Luke 21:20)

No Ordinary Curtains

1. **OSLPO**
2. **NTLERBCAEA**
3. **NNILE**
4. **TUBCI**
5. **TNKO**
6. **SMSOE**
7. **ACMONDM**

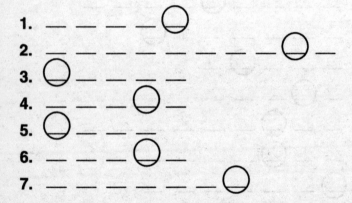

1. — — — — ⊝
2. — — — — — — — — ⊝ —
3. ⊝ — — — — —
4. — — ⊝ — —
5. ⊝ — — —
6. — — — ⊝ —
7. — — — — — — ⊝

"All the ⊝⊝⊝⊝⊝⊝⊝ men among the workmen made the tabernacle with ten curtains of finely twisted linen and blue, purple and scarlet yarn, with cherubim worked into them by a skilled craftsman."

(Exodus 36:8)

What a Great Guy!

1. **LAKOC**
2. **DNDEMA**
3. **OINGRNM**
4. **MIULRCEF**
5. **RISEHAESP**
6. **KAENT**
7. **ATHBBSA**
8. **EARDWR**

1. — — — ◯ —
2. — — ◯ — — —
3. — — — ◯ — — —
4. — — — — ◯ — — —
5. — — ◯ — — ◯ — — —
6. — ◯ — — —
7. — — — — ◯ —
8. ◯ — — — — —

"But a ◯◯◯◯◯◯◯◯, as he traveled, came where the man was; and when he saw him, he took pity on him."

(Luke 10:33)

A Dull Glow

1. **RABLEAP**
2. **NFIULS**
3. **IEARGNGTH**
4. **MSTUREOI**
5. **EARTMPDL**
6. **EORPNV**
7. **ISRBD**
8. **CTOCAUN**

1. — — — — — ⬭ —
2. — ⬭ — — — —
3. — ⬭ — — — — — — —
4. — — — — — — — ⬭
5. — — ⬭ — — — — —
6. — — ⬭ — — —
7. — — — ⬭ —
8. — ⬭ — — — —

One of the seven stars.

(Revelation 1:11)

A Leader's End

1. GHMYTI
2. AOPRMCLI
3. VADDI
4. HBTHMELEE
5. EISRKD
6. RPSAE
7. FDDENE
8. ONGHTROLSD
9. RGSIRAON
10. PXTSLOIE

1. _ Ⓞ _ _ _ _
2. Ⓞ _ _ _ _ _ _
3. _ _ Ⓞ _ _
4. _ _ _ Ⓞ _ _ Ⓞ _ _
5. _ _ Ⓞ _ _
6. Ⓞ _ _ _ _
7. _ _ _ Ⓞ _ _
8. _ _ _ _ Ⓞ _ _ _
9. _ _ _ Ⓞ _ _
10. _ _ _ _ _ Ⓞ _ _

The Ⓞ Ⓞ Ⓞ Ⓞ Ⓞ Ⓞ Ⓞ Ⓞ Ⓞ Ⓞ
found Saul and his sons fallen on Mount Gilboa.

(1 Samuel 31:8)

Powerful Men

1. DANSHOUT
2. AOOHDSFEL
3. MGEAO
4. ONUEINTC
5. ALSSG
6. GIRDNEE
7. NYDLEGII
8. AEUGLPS
9. NLIWGIL

1. ◯ _ _ _ _ _ _ _ _
2. _ _ _ ◯ _ _ _ _ _
3. _ _ ◯ _ _ _
4. _ _ _ _ _ _ _ ◯
5. _ _ _ ◯ _
6. _ _ _ _ ◯ _ _
7. _ _ _ _ _ ◯ _ _
8. _ _ _ _ _ _ ◯
9. ◯ _ _ _ _ _

Two of them could shut up the sky.

◯◯◯◯◯◯◯◯

(Revelation 11:3, 6)

Almighty Blood

1. **EENCERVER**
2. **RNTEEPS**
3. **GARDNO**
4. **UPATESHRE**
5. **SPLAE**
6. **MGNIUBLR**
7. **YJNIRU**
8. **MDSNOE**

1. — — — — — — ⊖ — —
2. — — — — — — ⊖
3. — — — — ⊖ —
4. ⊖ — — — — — — ⊖ — —
5. — — — — ⊖
6. — — — — — ⊖ — —
7. — — — — — ⊖
8. — — ⊖ — — —

"They overcame him by the blood of the Lamb

and by the word of their

⊖⊖⊖⊖⊖⊖⊖⊖⊖."

(Revelation 12:11)

Divine Farmers

1. **AHMEESPBL**
2. **TCERSPE**
3. **AAFLT**
4. **XISEERCE**
5. **HTOUFG**
6. **TWARH**
7. **EGVIN**

1. _ _ _ _ _ _ Ⓞ _ _

2. Ⓞ _ _ _ _ _ _

3. _ _ Ⓞ _ _

4. _ _ _ Ⓞ _ _ _ _

5. _ _ _ _ Ⓞ _

6. _ _ Ⓞ _ _

7. _ _ Ⓞ _ _

The time has come for the

Ⓞ Ⓞ Ⓞ Ⓞ Ⓞ Ⓞ of the earth.

(Revelation 14:15)

Worst of Horrors

---

1. **HISTRPA**
2. **EANLG**
3. **MENUODREST**
4. **EFLLDI**
5. **LOSTNESAHI**
6. **ISKGN**
7. **EAVELR**
8. **FWLLOO**

1. _ ◯ _ _ _ _ _

2. ◯ _ _ _ _

3. _ _ _ ◯ _ _ ◯ _ _ _

4. _ _ _ _ _ ◯ _

5. _ _ _ _ _ _ _ ◯ ◯ _

6. _ _ _ ◯ _

7. ◯ _ _ _ _ _

8. _ _ _ _ ◯ _

Not a good place to be.

(Revelation 16:16)

How about Some Faith?

1. AHPAHOR
2. NBDLI
3. HWPRSIO
4. NNACAA
5. NJGDTUME

6. MAINTUNO
7. ASLEIRTEI
8. CRCEFIASI
9. OQATU
10. TCTERAS

1. _ _ _ Ⓞ _ _ _
2. _ Ⓞ _ _ _
3. _ Ⓞ _ _ _ _ _
4. _ _ _ _ Ⓞ _ _
5. _ _ _ _ Ⓞ _ _ _
6. _ _ Ⓞ _ _ _ _
7. _ _ _ _ _ Ⓞ _ _
8. Ⓞ _ _ _ _ _ _ _
9. _ Ⓞ _ _ _
10. _ Ⓞ _ _ _ _ _

"Then the LORD said, 'If they do not believe you or pay attention to the first

Ⓞ Ⓞ Ⓞ Ⓞ Ⓞ Ⓞ Ⓞ Ⓞ Ⓞ sign,

they may believe the second.' "

(Exodus 4:8)

92

Hidden Wisdom

1. AEELDLCR
2. ENDADM
3. THTUYIRAO
4. ABIBR
5. IBLDU
6. FNDUO
7. OUGRBHT
8. SAIDHTEAB
9. ELEBVIE
10. STONYMITE

1. _ _ _ ◯ _ _ _ _
2. _ ◯ _ _ _ _
3. _ _ _ _ _ ◯ _ _ _
4. _ _ _ ◯ _
5. _ ◯ _ _ _
6. ◯ _ _ _ _
7. _ _ _ ◯ _ _
8. _ ◯ _ _ _ _ _ _
9. _ _ _ _ ◯ _ _
10. _ _ _ _ ◯ _ _ _

A way of not speaking plainly.

◯◯◯◯◯◯◯◯◯◯

language   (John 16:25)

Righteous Celebration

1. TARNEEL
2. LPICESDIS
3. ASBITRIE
4. NAANM
5. SLNSEU
6. ANGIZAM
7. USRECAC
8. BMRUGEDL
9. NTONHIG
10. CERALED

1. _ O _ _ _ _ _
2. _ _ _ _ O _ _ _ _
3. _ _ _ O _ _ _ _
4. _ _ _ _ O _
5. _ O _ _ _ _
6. _ _ _ _ O _ _
7. _ O _ _ _ _ _
8. _ _ _ _ _ _ O _
9. _ O _ _ _ _ _
10. O _ _ _ _ _ _

"Then came the Feast of

O O O O O O O O O at

Jerusalem."

(John 10:22)

94

Dearly Loved

1. **YEBANTH**
2. **EINDNR**
3. **IEENCLR**
4. **CARIOSIT**
5. **BUTSLEM**
6. **OEAZSUL**
7. **AANCEGRRF**

1. ＿ ＿ ＿ ＿ ◯ ＿ ＿
2. ＿ ＿ ＿ ＿ ◯ ＿
3. ＿ ＿ ◯ ＿ ＿ ＿
4. ＿ ◯ ＿ ＿ ＿ ＿ ＿
5. ＿ ＿ ◯ ＿ ＿ ＿
6. ◯ ＿ ＿ ＿ ＿ ＿ ＿
7. ＿ ＿ ＿ ＿ ＿ ◯ ＿ ＿ ＿

"Meanwhile a large crowd of Jews found out that Jesus was there and came, not only because of him but also to see ◯◯◯◯◯◯, whom he had raised from the dead."

(John 12:9)

The Wonder of the Lord

1. ERDONSLP
2. STTRU
3. SVNATRE
4. TRHFEA
5. SOPROPRSSE

6. REDPI
7. EOBTWS
8. SENCEEPR
9. FEMLRCUI

1. _ _ _ _ _ _ _ _
2. _ _ _ _ _
3. _ _ _ _ _ _ _
4. _ _ _ _ _ _
5. _ _ _ _ _ _ _ _ _
6. _ _ _ _ _
7. _ _ _ _ _ _
8. _ _ _ _ _ _ _
9. _ _ _ _ _ _ _

"Praise be to the LORD, for he showed his

◯◯◯◯◯◯◯◯ love to me

when I was in a besieged city."

(Psalm 31:21)

96

Looking Far

1. **ONBUD**
2. **PPELRU**
3. **TTORECP**
4. **JEDETBCO**
5. **ENEDDI**
6. **NOILEBELR**
7. **ITALEP**

1. — — — — ⬤

2. — — — ⬤ — —

3. — — — — ⬤ —

4. — — ⬤ — — — —

5. — — — ⬤ — —

6. ⬤ — — — — — — —

7. — — — ⬤ —

Seeing that which is ahead.

(1 Samuel 28:17)

The End Is Near

1. **AEIMCRL**
2. **DRGADEG**
3. **NHSIGIF**
4. **DUSCEMINO**
5. **RLOSIED**
6. **OIREPMSSNI**
7. **EGNIV**
8. **EAPPRER**

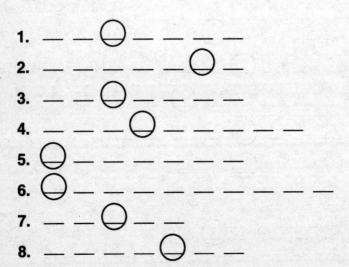

Just before this, Jesus knew it was time to leave.

(Exodus 12:27)

98

Love Kiss

1. TRASI
2. ENDEID
3. ALERCD
4. HRTAE
5. RVLOUAESM
6. EEVOTDD
7. OTRHF
8. ROUSUIF
9. ASURETP
10. GHSITR

1. _ _ _ ◯ _
2. _ ◯ _ _ ◯ _
3. _ _ ◯ _ _ _
4. ◯ _ _ _ _
5. _ _ _ _ _ ◯ _ ◯ _
6. _ _ _ _ ◯ _ _ _
7. ◯ _ _ _ _
8. ◯ _ _ _ _ _
9. _ _ ◯ _ _ _
10. _ _ _ _ ◯

"Love and

◯◯◯◯◯◯◯◯◯◯◯◯

meet together; righteousness and peace kiss each

other."

(Psalm 85:10)

99

Skill over Dull

1. **RMEDHAC**
2. **OURACISG**
3. **TLEATB**
4. **TIPULLIMES**
5. **DMESSAN**
6. **OASDWH**
7. **ERVESED**

1. ⊖ _ _ _ _ _ _

2. _ _ _ ⊖ _ _ _ _

3. _ _ _ _ ⊖

4. _ ⊖ _ _ _ _ _ _ _ _

5. _ _ _ _ _ _ ⊖

6. ⊖ _ _ _ _

7. _ _ ⊖ _ _ _

"If the ax is dull and its edge unsharpened, more strength is needed but skill will bring

"

(Ecclesiastes 10:10)

A Huge Catch

1. OHRAITC
2. AGEHRT
3. MOSACNISPO
4. MFESLA
5. BRKEUE
6. RRPAYE
7. HRABET
8. RFVEREO
9. VLEO

1. _ _ _ _ ◯ _ _
2. _ _ _ ◯ _ _
3. _ _ _ _ _ _ _ _ _ _ ◯ _
4. _ _ ◯ _ _ _
5. _ ◯ _ _ _ _
6. _ _ ◯ _ _ _ _
7. _ _ _ _ ◯ _ _
8. _ _ _ _ ◯ _ _
9. ◯ _ _ _

He's really big and loves to frolic.

◯◯◯◯◯◯◯◯◯

(Psalm 104:25–26)

Growing Nicely

1. TBEARH
2. AUWRDP
3. NREIDSF
4. NAPPHE
5. JENTNYMEO

6. OORLNCT
7. EALUFUTIB
8. NILETS
9. DAIRSPE
10. VNCAER

1. _ Ⓞ _ _ _ _
2. _ _ _ _ Ⓞ _
3. _ _ _ _ _ Ⓞ
4. _ _ _ Ⓞ _ _
5. _ _ Ⓞ _ _ _ _
6. _ _ _ Ⓞ _ _ _
7. _ _ _ _ Ⓞ _ _ _
8. _ _ _ Ⓞ _ _
9. _ _ Ⓞ _ _ _
10. _ _ Ⓞ _ _ _

God made these to water groves of flourishing trees.

Ⓞ Ⓞ Ⓞ Ⓞ Ⓞ Ⓞ Ⓞ Ⓞ Ⓞ Ⓞ

(Ecclesiastes 2:6)

Running in Place

1. **EUGMNDJT**
2. **JCTSOPRE**
3. **LRISHOUF**
4. **SDWIMO**
5. **NBRDUE**
6. **EEUDRN**
7. **EERVER**
8. **GRHTAITS**

1. _ _ _ _ _ ◯ _ _

2. _ _ ◯ _ _ _ _ _

3. _ _ _ _ _ _ ◯ _

4. _ ◯ _ _ _ _

5. _ ◯ _ _ _ _

6. _ _ _ _ ◯ _

7. _ _ ◯ _ _ _

8. _ _ _ _ _ ◯ _ _

"So I hated life, because the work that is done under the sun was ◯◯◯◯◯◯◯◯ to me. All of it is meaningless, a chasing after the wind."

(Ecclesiastes 2:17)

Serenade

1. OEVLR
2. NARDEYSVI
3. EANOBNL
4. WNGOILF
5. AFNTINOU
6. WESJEL
7. AINUNTMO

1. Ⓞ _ _ _ _
2. _ _ Ⓞ _ _ _ _ _ _
3. _ _ _ _ _ Ⓞ _ _
4. _ _ Ⓞ _ _ _ _
5. _ Ⓞ _ _ _ _ _ _
6. _ _ _ _ _ Ⓞ
7. Ⓞ _ _ _ _ _ _

He wrote a book of love.

Ⓞ Ⓞ Ⓞ Ⓞ Ⓞ Ⓞ Ⓞ

Lookout

1. **NAHESLD**
2. **VAPTCIE**
3. **ETWORS**
4. **DDCENSE**
5. **LACEUFGR**
6. **AIWTS**
7. **SRAFMANTC**
8. **MTCIJSAE**

1. ◯ __ __ __ __ __ __
2. __ __ __ __ __ __ ◯
3. ◯ __ __ __ __ __
4. __ __ __ __ __ ◯ __
5. __ __ ◯ __ __ __ __ __
6. ◯ __ __ __ __
7. ◯ __ __ __ __ __ __ __ __
8. ◯ __ __ __ __ __ __

"The ◯◯◯◯◯◯◯ found me as they made their rounds in the city."

(Song of Songs 5:7)

105

Ouch!

1. **OERNRC**
2. **BNIGHORE**
3. **SUTCNTRI**
4. **OURRPCT**
5. **ROTPOFOS**
6. **TIEABNG**
7. **OOVERLOK**
8. **RLURAQE**

1. ___ ___ ___ ⬭ ___ ___

2. ___ ⬭ ___ ___ ___ ___ ___ ___

3. ⬭ ___ ___ ___ ___ ___ ___ ___

4. ___ ___ ___ ___ ___ ___ ⬭ ___

5. ___ ___ ___ ___ ___ ⬭ ___ ___ ⬭

6. ___ ⬭ ___ ___ ___ ___ ___

7. ___ ___ ___ ___ ⬭ ___ ___ ___

8. ___ ___ ⬭ ___ ___ ___ ___

"⬭⬭⬭⬭⬭⬭⬭⬭ are prepared for mockers, and beatings for the backs of fools."

(Proverbs 19:29)

Talking of the Future

1. LUCOSROEN
2. NMNDKIA
3. PTBAEIZ
4. EEJRMSLAU
5. EDXTLAE

6. TDRSIESA
7. FFTHILUA
8. ERSAREUT
9. COALSFIFI
10. NHROO

1. _ _ _ _○_ _ _ _
2. _○_ _ _ _ _
3. _ _ _ _○_ _
4. _ _ _ _ _ _ _ _○
5. _ _○_ _ _ _
6. _○_ _ _ _ _ _
7. _ _○_ _ _ _ _
8. _ _ _○_ _ _ _
9. ○_ _ _ _ _ _ _
10. ○_ _ _ _ _

God spoke to ○○○○○○ son of
○○○○ of what was to come.

(2 Kings 20:1)

Round and Round

1. **SIDESLNE**
2. **VRGIO**
3. **RNTSMAGE**
4. **UARPSSS**
5. **TMERBLE**
6. **NFDECENIOC**
7. **GDTANRI**
8. **WSSDOR**

1. _ _ _ _ ◯ _ _ _
2. _ ◯ _ _ _
3. _ _ _ _ _ _ _ ◯ _
4. ◯ _ _ _ _ _ _
5. ◯ _ _ _ _ _ _
6. _ _ _ ◯ _ _ _ _
7. _ _ _ _ _ ◯
8. _ ◯ _ _ _ _

"For as churning the milk produces butter, and as ◯◯◯◯◯◯◯ the nose produces blood, so stirring up anger produces strife."

Eyes in the Dark

1. HTRIGENF
2. CNNTIEA
3. ATRPSA
4. BENSCRII
5. EANDTT
6. URWPOEFL
7. STFUOALB
8. AELAZB

1. _ _ _ _ _ _ _ ⊖
2. _ ⊖ _ _ _ _ _
3. ⊖ _ _ _ _ _
4. _ _ _ _ ⊖ _ _
5. _ _ _ _ ⊖
6. _ ⊖ _ _ _ _ _
7. _ _ _ _ _ _ ⊖
8. _ _ _ _ _ ⊖

In this deep and dark place could Daniel be found.

⊖⊖⊖⊖⊖' ⊖⊖⊖

(Daniel 6:16)

Follow and Learn

1. NSIOFENCOS
2. OERSPC
3. EIPLDCRP
4. CNTAIER

5. TTDSEE
6. RSPTEAEA
7. EULYDSDN
8. EUDPSARE

1. ◯ — — — — — — — —
2. — — — — — ◯
3. — ◯ — — — — —
4. — — — ◯ — —
5. — — — — ◯
6. ◯ — — — — — — —
7. ◯ — — — — — ◯
8. ◯ — — — — — —

They wondered why some people were so difficult to heal.

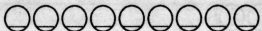

(Matthew 17:18–20)

A Greater Love

1. CILNCUO
2. TSABALARE
3. TLEDGHI
4. AAGEIMRR
5. TCREHEA

6. ONBNTMIAIOA
7. WNAOM
8. RMFI
9. DNPAHEPE
10. MRROU

1. __ __ __ Ⓞ __ __ __

2. __ __ Ⓞ __ __ Ⓞ __ __ __

3. Ⓞ __ __ __ __ Ⓞ

4. __ __ __ __ __ __ __ __ Ⓞ

5. __ __ __ Ⓞ __ __ __

6. __ __ __ Ⓞ __ __ __ __ __ __ __

7. __ Ⓞ __ __ __

8. __ __ __ Ⓞ

9. __ __ __ __ __ Ⓞ __ __

10. __ __ Ⓞ __ __

No greater than these, to love God and your neighbor.

ⓄⓄⓄⓄⓄⓄⓄⓄⓄⓄⓄⓄ

(Exodus 20:1–17)

On to the Cross

1. DERUOL
2. RMEDA
3. RIFIEDUCC
4. RABAABSB
5. EAONTMIPTT
6. URTARDCOY
7. HERNOTA
8. PROVESAS
9. ONGDKIM
10. DARGUED

1. _ ◯ _ _ _ _
2. _ _ ◯ _ _
3. _ _ _ _ _ _ _ ◯ _
4. _ _ _ ◯ _ _ _ _
5. _ _ _ _ _ _ ◯ _ _ _
6. _ _ _ _ _ _ _ ◯ _
7. _ _ _ _ _ _ ◯
8. ◯ _ _ _ _ _ _ _
9. _ ◯ _ _ _ _ _
10. _ ◯ _ _ _ _ _

"The soldiers led Jesus away into the palace (that is, the ◯◯◯◯◯◯◯◯◯) and called together the whole company of soldiers."

(Mark 15:16)

What a Sight!

1. WBLNROO
2. RNPEOS
3. TVRYCIO
4. EANCSRIE
5. LNCEBAA
6. LSTNOE
7. THSOU
8. VTNOSLAIA
9. NSLADA

1. _ _ _ _ _ Ⓞ _
2. _ _ _ Ⓞ _ _
3. _ _ _ _ _ _ Ⓞ
4. _ Ⓞ _ _ _ _ _
5. _ _ _ _ Ⓞ _
6. _ Ⓞ _ _ _
7. _ _ _ Ⓞ _
8. _ Ⓞ _ _ _ _ _ _ _
9. _ _ _ Ⓞ _

"I have seen you in the

Ⓞ Ⓞ Ⓞ Ⓞ Ⓞ Ⓞ Ⓞ Ⓞ Ⓞ and beheld

your power and your glory."

(Psalm 63:2)

Scary!

1. **BEADHEED**
2. **DULLOY**
3. **DEEGBG**
4. **PINROS**
5. **SFRGNEFUI**
6. **BEPRALA**
7. **QLLUSA**
8. **SCRHABEN**

1. — ◯ — — — ◯ — —
2. — ◯ — — — —
3. — — — ◯ — —
4. — — — ◯ — —
5. ◯ — — — — — — — —
6. ◯ — — — — — —
7. ◯ — — — — —
8. — — — — — — ◯

No longer your own person.

◯◯◯◯◯◯◯◯

(Matthew 4:24)

A Precious Act

1. **TUGGRINGLS**
2. **COTEV**
3. **MAPSBIT**
4. **NSGRRAESTS**
5. **CRAGE**
6. **LWLAUF**
7. **EETPRN**
8. **RISEMOP**

1. __ __ __ __ __ __ Ⓞ __ __ __

2. __ Ⓞ __ __ __

3. __ __ __ __ __ Ⓞ __

4. __ Ⓞ __ __ __ __ Ⓞ __ __

5. __ __ __ __ Ⓞ

6. __ __ Ⓞ __ __ __

7. __ __ Ⓞ __ __ __

8. __ __ __ __ __ Ⓞ __

"You see, at just the right time, when we were still

Ⓞ Ⓞ Ⓞ Ⓞ Ⓞ Ⓞ Ⓞ Ⓞ, Christ died

for the ungodly."

(Romans 5:6)

115

New Life

1. PINGFORFS
2. DOCE
3. RMCICUSEIC
4. RUSTNETED
5. RANTEU

6. REDGUG
7. CDTDRIEE
8. VRWAE
9. NTIBALOOIG
10. EAEDRLES

1. _ _ _ _ _ _ ⊖ _ _ _
2. ⊖ _ _ _ _
3. _ _ _ _ _ _ ⊖ _ _ _
4. _ _ _ _ _ _ _ _ ⊖
5. ⊖ _ _ _ _ _ _
6. _ _ _ _ _ ⊖ _
7. _ _ _ _ ⊖ _ _ _
8. _ _ _ ⊖ _
9. ⊖ _ _ _ _ _ _ _ _
10. _ _ ⊖ _ _ _ _

"For if, when we were God's enemies, we were

⊖⊖⊖⊖⊖⊖⊖⊖⊖ to him

through the death of his Son, how much more,
having been reconciled, shall we be saved through
his life!"

(Romans 5:10)

116

Not Good!

1. APNNLDE
2. MSNOMU
3. LDFIDEE
4. VTELOIA
5. KRNOBE

6. MNCOSEU
7. RETAH
8. RDGACESI
9. SOLEOCN

1. ◯ — — — — — —
2. — ◯ — — — — —
3. — — — — — — ◯
4. — — — ◯ — — —
5. — ◯ — — — —
6. — — ◯ — — — —
7. ◯ — — — —
8. ◯ — — — — — —
9. — — — — — ◯

"The earth will be completely laid waste and totally ◯◯◯◯◯◯◯◯◯. The LORD has spoken this word."

(Isaiah 24:3)

117

Loving Care

---

1. NGUDIJG
2. DHUTOCE
3. EIONRG
4. SENYLRT
5. ROODNIS

6. TEENRAINT
7. SINYO
8. SEWNIKIN
9. AYRCR
10. RICEPACT

1. __ __ __ __ __ Ⓞ
2. __ Ⓞ __ __ __ __ __
3. Ⓞ __ __ __ __ __
4. __ __ __ Ⓞ __ __ __ __
5. __ Ⓞ __ __ __ __
6. Ⓞ __ __ __ __ __ __ __ __
7. __ __ Ⓞ __ __
8. __ __ Ⓞ __ __ __ __
9. Ⓞ __ __ __ __
10. __ __ __ __ __ Ⓞ __

He speaks to His angels

Ⓞ Ⓞ Ⓞ Ⓞ Ⓞ Ⓞ Ⓞ Ⓞ Ⓞ Ⓞ us,

for our sake.

(Psalm 91:11)

Need a Lawyer?

1. OLFISHO
2. RAYTLICAP
3. AUEDLGH
4. MADEAZ
5. BUREDEK
6. RMCYE
7. HEARTSV
8. DEAPSR

1. _ _ _ _ _ Ⓞ _
2. _ Ⓞ _ _ _ Ⓞ _ _ _
3. _ Ⓞ _ _ _ _ _
4. _ _ _ Ⓞ _
5. Ⓞ _ _ _ _ _
6. _ _ Ⓞ _ _
7. _ _ _ Ⓞ _ _ _
8. _ _ _ _ _ Ⓞ

" 'Settle matters quickly with your

ⓄⓄⓄⓄⓄⓄⓄⓄ who is taking
you to court.' "

(Matthew 5:25)

119

The Extra Step

1. BEDSSEL
2. RSUTECEEP
3. RICEEJO
4. NOWINW
5. NUTSIL
6. RPEHTOP
7. HUMOT

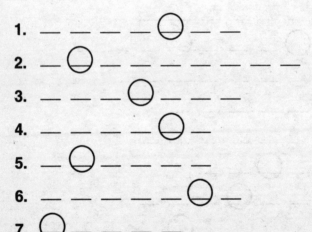

1. _ _ _ _ Ⓞ _ _

2. _ Ⓞ _ _ _ _ _ _ _

3. _ _ Ⓞ _ _ _

4. _ _ _ Ⓞ _ _

5. Ⓞ _ _ _ _

6. _ _ _ _ Ⓞ _

7. Ⓞ _ _ _ _

" 'If ⓄⓄⓄⓄⓄⓄ forces you to go one mile, go with him two miles.' "

(Matthew 5:41)

An Honest Gift

1. LASHYMEPB   6. HDDNEI
2. ASHGIGNN   7. AEIVRSR
3. SWEDO   8. CERPIEVE
4. PALER   9. SLARECES
5. AUNTOM   10. WETRIH

1. __ __ __ __ __ __ __ __◯
2. __ __ __◯ __ __ __
3. __◯ __ __ __
4. ◯ __ __ __
5. __ __ __ __◯
6. ◯ __ __ __ __
7. __ __◯ __ __ __
8. __ __ __◯ __
9. ◯ __ __ __ __ __ __
10. __◯ __ __ __ __

" 'So when you give to the needy, do not announce it with trumpets, as the

◯◯◯◯◯◯◯◯◯◯ do in the synagogues and on the streets, to be honored by men.' "

(Matthew 6:2)

121

Moving On

1. ROTNTCIE
2. HFLRSOUI
3. AMMEIROL
4. HELITGD
5. NDHIDE
6. BCNANDUAE
7. TYWOHR
8. VLTEIE
9. XDTENE
10. NLASI

1. _ _ _ _ _ _ _〇
2. _ _ _ _ _ _〇_
3. _〇_ _ _ _ _ _
4. _〇_ _ _ _ _
5. 〇_ _ _ _ _
6. _ _ _〇_ _ _ _ _
7. 〇_ _ _ _ _
8. _ _〇_ _ _
9. _ _ _ _〇_ _
10. _ _〇_ _

"Behold, I will create new 〇〇〇〇〇〇〇 and a 〇〇〇 earth. The former things will not be remembered, nor will they come to mind."

(Isaiah 65:17)

Too Many Words

1. **SLEDOO**
2. **CLRENHID**
3. **BOHERTR**
4. **GILLWIN**
5. **RAWDEN**
6. **NAGAP**
7. **BUDON**
8. **TRIGBHYL**

1. Ⓞ _ _ _ _ _

2. _ _ _ _ _ _ _ Ⓞ _

3. Ⓞ _ _ _ _ _ _

4. _ _ _ _ Ⓞ _ _

5. _ Ⓞ _ _ _ _

6. _ _ Ⓞ _ _

7. Ⓞ _ _ _ _

8. Ⓞ _ _ _ _ _ _ _

" 'And when you pray, do not keep on

ⓄⓄⓄⓄⓄⓄⓄ like pagans, for
they think they will be heard because of their many
words.' "

(Matthew 6:7)

123

Honest Hunger

1. YJFLOU
2. SINGFAT
3. TUBROLE
4. HRFREOEET

5. WASTSUD
6. OYRLG
7. RHLYGIT
8. SIDESEP

1. _ _ _ _ Ⓞ _
2. _ _ Ⓞ _ _ _
3. _ Ⓞ _ _ _ _ Ⓞ
4. _ _ _ _ _ _ Ⓞ _ _ _
5. _ _ _ Ⓞ _ _ _
6. Ⓞ _ _ _ _
7. _ Ⓞ _ _ _ _
8. _ _ _ _ Ⓞ _ _

" 'When you fast, do not look somber as the hypocrites do, for they

Ⓞ Ⓞ Ⓞ Ⓞ Ⓞ Ⓞ Ⓞ Ⓞ their faces to show men they are fasting.' "

(Matthew 6:16)

Faulty Towers

1. **SENDLORP**
2. **RATEGONENI**
3. **NODMONII**
4. **CMISU**
5. **TEAMDIET**
6. **GASTNIL**
7. **REPESHDH**
8. **DEALCL**

1. — — — — — — —Ⓞ
2. — —Ⓞ— — — — — —
3. — — — — —Ⓞ— —
4. — — —Ⓞ— — —
5. — — — —Ⓞ— —
6. — —Ⓞ— — —
7. — —Ⓞ— — — —
8. Ⓞ— — — — —

" 'But everyone who hears these words of mine and does not put them into

Ⓞ Ⓞ Ⓞ Ⓞ Ⓞ Ⓞ Ⓞ Ⓞ   is like a foolish man who built his house on sand.' "

(Matthew 7:26)

125

In God's Way

1. **NWSTEIS**
2. **EAGHTDUR**
3. **CRSEUE**
4. **RUCYONT**
5. **NHINRASDE**
6. **PEYTG**
7. **MFNEAI**
8. **FMRPREO**

1. __ __ __ __ Ⓞ __ __
2. __ __ __ __ __ __ Ⓞ
3. __ Ⓞ __ __ __ __ __
4. __ __ Ⓞ __ __ __
5. __ __ __ __ Ⓞ __ __ __
6. Ⓞ __ __ __ __
7. Ⓞ __ __ __ __ __
8. __ __ __ __ __ __ Ⓞ

The members of the Synagogue of the

ⒶⒷⒸⒹⒺⒻⒼⒽ opposed

Stephen.

(Acts 6:9–10)

Always Faithful

1. SOONIP
2. RENAS
3. BEALTT
4. NOWVE
5. LAREDSN
6. SUNDRORU
7. VEARYRADS

1. _ _ _ _ Ⓞ _
2. _ Ⓞ _ _ _
3. Ⓞ _ _ _ _
4. _ _ _ _ Ⓞ
5. _ _ Ⓞ _ _ _ _
6. _ _ _ _ _ _ _ Ⓞ
7. Ⓞ _ _ _ _ _ _ _ _

"The Lᴏʀᴅ will fulfill his purpose for me; your love, O Lᴏʀᴅ, endures forever—do not Ⓞ Ⓞ Ⓞ Ⓞ Ⓞ Ⓞ Ⓞ the works of your hands."

(Psalm 138:8)

A Dark Night

1. **ROBTIRNSF**
2. **NORDHEETN**
3. **TANUBDAN**
4. **WORDSNE**
5. **PIONSIRVO**
6. **LAIIFUNGN**
7. **ERITSPYROP**
8. **AISERP**

1. _ _ _ _ O _ _ _ _
2. _ O _ _ _ _ _ _ _
3. _ O _ _ _ _ _ _
4. _ _ O _ _ _ _
5. O _ _ _ _ _ _ _ _
6. _ _ _ _ _ _ _ _ O
7. _ _ _ _ _ _ _ O _ _
8. _ _ _ O _ _

"When I was in distress, I sought the Lord; at night I stretched out O O O O O O O hands and my soul refused to be comforted."

(Psalm 77:2)

128

Words from God

1. **WINGSVER**
2. **DEAPCHR**
3. **COFERS**
4. **BENDUR**
5. **SEALUJO**
6. **OETHNRRN**
7. **SOTLEJ**

1. _ _ ◯ _ _ _ _ _

2. ◯ _ _ _ _ _ _

3. _ _ _ _ ◯ _

4. _ ◯ _ _ _ _

5. _ _ ◯ _ _ _

6. _ _ _ _ ◯ _ _ _

7. _ _ _ ◯ _ _

"The word of the LORD that came to Joel son of  ◯◯◯◯◯◯."

(Joel 1:1)

Free in Christ

1. ERITNTW
2. SNGTEELI
3. DPRETUE
4. ELAYSRV
5. RANEBR

6. ESLZAUO
7. PPSERUO
8. TRSPII
9. LGNSTIAAA
10. PLSGEO

1. _ _ _ _ _ _Ⓞ
2. _ _ _ _Ⓞ _ _ _
3. Ⓞ _ _ _ _ _ _
4. _ _ _Ⓞ _ _ _ _
5. _ _ _ _Ⓞ _ _
6. _ _ _ _ _Ⓞ _
7. Ⓞ _ _ _Ⓞ _ _
8. Ⓞ _ _ _ _ _
9. _ _ _ _ _Ⓞ _ _
10. _ _Ⓞ _ _ _

"Now that faith has come, we are no longer under

the Ⓞ Ⓞ Ⓞ Ⓞ Ⓞ Ⓞ Ⓞ Ⓞ Ⓞ Ⓞ

of the law."

(Galatians 3:25)

130

Family of God

1. **NERSDIC**
2. **OYLFL**
3. **EEFADTNT**
4. **SAMLC**
5. **MASHFUEL**
6. **RTFLUHUT**
7. **EORCKM**
8. **BUTEJCS**

1. — — — ⦵ — — — —
2. — — — ⦵ —
3. — — — — — — — ⦵
4. — — — — ⦵
5. — — ⦵ — — — —
6. — ⦵ — — — — —
7. — — — — ⦵ —
8. — — — — ⦵ — —

" 'At that time,' ⦵⦵⦵⦵⦵⦵⦵

the LORD, 'I will be the God of all the clans of Israel,
and they will be my people.' "

(Jeremiah 31:1)

131

Unwanted

1. SALESEP
2. UGHHATY
3. NOBAIT
4. SIDECORN
5. TEERSC
6. HOSESOT
7. ELATHW
8. HYNURG
9. RPOEHCRA

1. _ _ _ _ _ Ⓞ _
2. Ⓞ _ _ _ _ _ _
3. _ Ⓞ _ _ _ _
4. _ _ _ _ _ _ _ Ⓞ
5. _ _ _ _ Ⓞ _
6. _ Ⓞ _ _ _ _ _
7. _ _ Ⓞ _ _ _
8. _ _ Ⓞ _ _ _
9. _ _ _ Ⓞ _ _ _ _

Jeremiah tells of a time when the people of God
will be Ⓞ Ⓞ Ⓞ Ⓞ Ⓞ Ⓞ Ⓞ Ⓞ to all
the kingdoms of the earth.

(Jeremiah 15:4)

132

Food for the Heart

1. **LSSNHIOE**
2. **NRSPOI**
3. **PCAEE**
4. **TTDETESIU**
5. **EHDLAE**

6. **TMCUOOE**
7. **TEMTIIA**
8. **ASGDCREI**
9. **JYNEO**
10. **AASCI**

1. — — — — — ◯ — —
2. — — ◯ — — —
3. — — ◯ — — —
4. — — — — — — — — ◯
5. — — — ◯ — —
6. ◯ — — — — — —
7. — ◯ — — — — —
8. — — — — ◯ — — —
9. — ◯ — — — —
10. — — — — ◯

"It is good for our hearts to be strengthened by grace, not by ◯◯◯◯◯◯◯◯◯◯ foods, which are of no value to those who eat them."

(Hebrews 13:9)

What a Catch!

1. EORPPUS
2. RIBEB
3. USITECJ
4. FACESIPI
5. POSTMU
6. ERORTR
7. LEARVG
8. DOWNGEELK

1. $\_$ $\bigcirc$ $\_$ $\_$ $\_$ $\_$ $\_$

2. $\_$ $\_$ $\bigcirc$ $\_$ $\_$

3. $\_$ $\_$ $\_$ $\_$ $\bigcirc$ $\_$

4. $\_$ $\bigcirc$ $\_$ $\_$ $\_$ $\_$ $\bigcirc$

5. $\bigcirc$ $\_$ $\bigcirc$ $\_$ $\_$ $\_$

6. $\_$ $\_$ $\_$ $\bigcirc$ $\_$

7. $\_$ $\bigcirc$ $\_$ $\_$ $\_$ $\_$

8. $\_$ $\_$ $\_$ $\_$ $\bigcirc$ $\_$ $\_$ $\_$ $\_$

A $\bigcirc$ $\bigcirc$ $\bigcirc$ $\bigcirc$ $\bigcirc$ $\bigcirc$ $\bigcirc$ $\bigcirc$ $\bigcirc$ $\bigcirc$

catch of fish.

(John 21:1–6)

On the Journey

1. **HRUMLPATI**
2. **CISELPDIS**
3. **RNDEASIU**
4. **RRPEAPE**
5. **TREGA**
6. **CHTERAE**
7. **TRASME**
8. **BTRESI**
9. **HTROPPE**

1. ◯ _ _ _ _ _ _ _ _
2. _ _ _ _ _ _ _ ◯ _
3. _ ◯ _ _ _ _ _ _
4. ◯ _ _ _ _ _ _
5. ◯ _ _ _ _
6. _ _ _ _ ◯ _ _
7. _ ◯ _ _ _ _
8. _ _ _ ◯ _ _
9. _ _ _ ◯ _ _

On the way to Jerusalem, Jesus and His disciples came to ◯ ◯ ◯ ◯ ◯ ◯ ◯ ◯ on the Mount of Olives.

(Matthew 21:1)

135

The New Has Come

1. **SERGIOUV**
2. **EELPOP**
3. **FEEBTIN**
4. **NINGAME**

5. **REXMEET**
6. **ETSANGRR**
7. **AVIDO**
8. **DLGTHIE**

1. __ ⊖ __ __ __ __ __ ⊖

2. __ ⊖ __ __ __ __

3. __ __ ⊖ __ __ __ __

4. ⊖ __ __ __ __ __ __

5. __ __ ⊖ __ __ __ __

6. ⊖ __ __ __ __ __ __ __

7. __ __ __ ⊖ __

8. __ __ __ ⊖ __ __ __

They spoke of a new covenant.

⊖ ⊖ ⊖ ⊖ ⊖ ⊖ ⊖ ⊖

(2 Corinthians 3:6)

Shining Bright

1. **CONSATI**
2. **AISTOBGN**
3. **ROFEVER**
4. **TIISCIVETA**
5. **FERNRIOI**
6. **TRDEEPN**
7. **ELFAS**
8. **WIGKLEAN**

1. — — — — — ⊖ —

2. — — ⊖ — — — — —

3. — — — — ⊖ — — —

4. — — — — — — — — ⊖

5. — — — — ⊖ — — —

6. — — — — — — ⊖

7. — — — ⊖ —

8. — — — ⊖ — — — —

"For you were once

⊖⊖⊖⊖⊖⊖⊖, but now you are

light in the Lord. Live as children of light."

(Ephesians 5:8)

137

Honestly Rich

1. **SCORNDIETI**
2. **ITRAGSHT**
3. **WHGIHAY**
4. **EXTAL**
5. **METPREED**
6. **RONSHT**
7. **OESPER**
8. **TRUDNEP**

1. ◯ _ _ _ _ _ _ _ _ _

2. _ _ _ ◯ _ _ _

3. _ _ _ _ ◯ _ _

4. _ _ _ ◯ _

5. _ _ _ _ _ _ ◯

6. _ _ _ _ ◯ _

7. ◯ _ _ _ _ _

8. _ _ _ _ ◯ _

"Dishonest money ◯ ◯ ◯ ◯ ◯ ◯ ◯ ◯

away, but he who gathers money little by little

makes it grow."

(Proverbs 13:11)

No Kidding Around!

1. GTONEU
2. USNDOW
3. NPTACEEI
4. TENELG
5. OOSHLIF

6. VSNEIOU
7. EROVTYP
8. GDLSAGUR
9. SBTOA
10. QLRRAUE

1. _ _ Ⓞ _ _ _
2. _ _ _ _ Ⓞ _ _
3. _ _ Ⓞ _ _ _ _ _
4. _ _ _ _ Ⓞ _
5. Ⓞ _ _ _ _ _
6. _ _ _ _ Ⓞ _
7. _ _ _ Ⓞ _ _
8. _ _ _ _ Ⓞ _ _
9. Ⓞ _ _ _ _
10. _ _ Ⓞ _ _ _ _

"Like a madman shooting

Ⓞ Ⓞ Ⓞ Ⓞ Ⓞ Ⓞ Ⓞ Ⓞ Ⓞ or

deadly arrows is a man who deceives his neighbor

and says, 'I was only joking!' "

(Proverbs 26:18–19)

A Godly View

1. GONGNIL
2. YLARSH
3. AERCHSES
4. TERPODUO
5. HTREAT
6. USCDEER
7. LUCRE

1. _ _ _ _ _ Ⓞ _
2. Ⓞ _ _ _ _ _
3. _ _ _ _ _ _ Ⓞ _
4. _ Ⓞ _ _ _ _ _ _
5. _ _ _ _ Ⓞ
6. _ _ _ _ _ _ Ⓞ
7. _ _ Ⓞ _ _

"A fool shows his annoyance at once, but a

ⓄⓄⓄⓄⓄⓄ man overlooks an

insult."

(Proverbs 12:16)

Keep It Honest

1. HAINSB
2. PAVETIC
3. EOPTMNCT
4. DULECIIR
5. RILDEBU
6. ERRTUN
7. ERDCEE
8. YOFTL

1. _ _ _ O _ _
2. O _ _ _ _ _ _
3. _ _ _ _ O _ _ _ _
4. _ _ _ _ _ _ O _
5. _ O _ _ _ _ _
6. _ _ O _ _ _
7. O _ _ _ _ O
8. _ _ O _ _

"Save me, O Lord, from lying lips and from
O O O O O O O O O tongues."

(Psalm 120:2)

141

A Place for Everyone

1. **AENLTSADW**
2. **HHDWILET**
3. **ARSEFTHE**
4. **ATESH**
5. **DPVIERO**
6. **EMADWO**
7. **CDOTHEL**
8. **MORPLACI**

1. — ⊖ — — — — — — — —

2. — — — — — ⊖ — — _

3. ⊖ — — — — — ⊖ — —

4. — — ⊖ — ⊖ —

5. — — — — ⊖ — — —

6. ⊖ — — — — —

7. — ⊖ — — — — —

8. — — — — — — ⊖ —

God puts the lonely in
⊖⊖⊖⊖⊖⊖⊖⊖.

(Psalm 68:6)

A Strong Father

1. SEETHADH
2. HERISCH
3. CAPYMONAC
4. CATERTS
5. EIWLLDNG
6. GEERUF
7. ANLLEF
8. DIFELL

1. __ __ __ __ __ __ Ⓞ
2. __ __ Ⓞ __ __ __ __
3. __ __ __ __ __ __ __ Ⓞ __
4. __ __ __ __ __ Ⓞ
5. Ⓞ __ __ __ __ __ __
6. __ __ __ __ Ⓞ __
7. __ __ __ Ⓞ __
8. Ⓞ __ __ __ __ __

"A father to the fatherless, a

Ⓞ Ⓞ Ⓞ Ⓞ Ⓞ Ⓞ Ⓞ Ⓞ of widows,

is God in his holy dwelling."

(Psalm 68:5)

Traveling Band

1. **ETPPDSIR**
2. **EOARFBOT**
3. **LFFCSAIOI**
4. **SEEPAC**
5. **NOKYSED**
6. **AGTRNSE**
7. **TIHGF**
8. **SOILD**

1. ◯ _ _ _ _ _ _ _
2. _ _ _ ◯ _ _ _ _
3. _ _ _ ◯ _ _ ◯ _ _
4. ◯ _ _ _ _ _
5. ◯ _ _ _ _ _ _
6. _ _ _ ◯ _ _
7. _ _ _ ◯ _
8. _ ◯ _ _ _

"An oracle concerning Arabia: You caravans of ◯◯◯◯◯◯◯◯, who camp in the thickets of Arabia."

(Isaiah 21:13)

Speak It Out!

1. GODEL
2. ASMNGEL
3. DADMNE
4. EHELEMBTH
5. SEEBACU
6. ALGNE
7. NHKPSIIG
8. UCHSR

1. _ ◯ _ _ _
2. ◯ _ _ _ _ _ _
3. _ _ _ _ ◯ _
4. _ _ ◯ _ _ _ _ _ _
5. _ _ _ ◯ _ ◯ _
6. _ _ _ _ ◯
7. _ ◯ _ _ _ _ _ _
8. _ _ ◯ _ _

"Listen to what the LORD says: 'Stand up, plead your case before the ◯◯◯◯◯◯◯◯◯; let the hills hear what you have to say.' "

(Micah 6:1)

145

Stay Committed

1. **DOOWGILL**
2. **ERPDATP**
3. **TCEEDI**
4. **HARSTEG**
5. **RENTPED**
6. **ACDVIE**
7. **IRHPES**
8. **NEETFIB**

1. _ _ _ _ _ _ _ _ ◯
2. ◯ _ _ _ _ _ _
3. ◯ _ _ _ _ _
4. ◯ _ _ _ _ _ _
5. _ _ ◯ _ _ _ _
6. _ _ _ ◯ _ _ _
7. _ _ _ ◯ _ _ _
8. _ _ ◯ _ _ _ _

"The sluggard craves and gets nothing, but the desires of the ◯◯◯◯◯◯◯ are fully satisfied."

(Proverbs 13:4)

Desert Preacher

1. SJUSE
2. ERPOTHPS
3. DHWSASO
4. SLDNAA
5. ZATPBEI
6. APALHNIT

7. REAABPL
8. PIRSTI
9. RESHSEIAP
10. UEDETBSATI
11. LSTA

1. Ⓞ — — — —
2. — — Ⓞ — — — — —
3. — Ⓞ — — — — — —
4. — Ⓞ — — — —
5. Ⓞ — — — — — —
6. — Ⓞ — — — —
7. Ⓞ — — — — — —
8. — — — — Ⓞ
9. — — — Ⓞ — — — —
10. — — — — — — — Ⓞ
11. — — Ⓞ —

He really lost his head over Jesus. Who was he?

Ⓞ Ⓞ Ⓞ Ⓞ the Ⓞ Ⓞ Ⓞ Ⓞ Ⓞ Ⓞ Ⓞ

(Matthew 14:8)

One of Seven

1. VERSEREPE
2. NGPASA
3. REHTRBO
4. TVERILENOA
5. NSIS
6. ELUSFSNL
7. LSPIEWFHLO

1. __ Ⓞ __ __ __ __ __ __ __
2. Ⓞ __ __ __ __ __
3. __ __ __ __ Ⓞ __ __
4. __ __ __ Ⓞ __ __ __ __ __ __
5. Ⓞ __ __ __
6. __ Ⓞ __ __ __ __ __ __
7. __ __ __ __ __ Ⓞ __ __ __

The church had a golden lampstand named after it.

ⓄⓄⓄⓄⓄⓄⓄ

(Revelation 1:20)

Jews Leave Rome

1. OPLEEP
2. IOGNRANG
3. NDSRCOEI
4. ROVGSEIEN
5. YRECM

6. FLINSU
7. GTESLURG
8. NTOLCOR
9. IPNSAOSS

1. __ __ __ Ⓞ __ __
2. __ Ⓞ __ __ __ __ __ __
3. __ __ __ __ Ⓞ __ __ __
4. Ⓞ __ __ __ __ __ __ __ __
5. __ __ __ Ⓞ __
6. __ Ⓞ __ __ __ __
7. __ __ __ __ __ Ⓞ __
8. __ __ __ __ __ __ Ⓞ
9. __ Ⓞ __ __ __ __ __ __

She may have had the same name, but she was
not the wife of the famous singer. Who was she?

(Acts 18:12)

Return to the Lord

1. ZAEBITP
2. NWEDOR
3. RCYESRO
4. TYHUO
5. RDCEEAL
6. RNESKTIC
7. LUYMPTIL
8. RAHTE
9. DHNSA

1. _ _ _ _ _ ⊖ _
2. _ _ _ _ ⊖ _
3. _ _ _ ⊖ _ _ _
4. _ _ _ ⊖ _
5. _ _ _ ⊖ _ _
6. _ _ ⊖ _ _ _ _ _
7. _ _ _ _ ⊖ _ _ _
8. _ ⊖ _ _ _
9. ⊖ _ _ _ _

This prophet was the son of Berekiah.

◯ ◯ ◯ ◯ ◯ ◯ ◯ ◯ ◯

(Zechariah 1:1)

Spirit-Filled

1. EPLEOP
2. ETARG
3. EISNAREC
4. ERERTOS
5. REUDVO

6. TOSUATC
7. ODBLEH
8. SAPS
9. TMSEI

1. ⊖ _ _ _ _ _
2. _ _ ⊖ _ _
3. _ ⊖ _ _ _ _ _ _
4. _ _ _ ⊖ _ _ _
5. _ ⊖ _ _ _ _
6. _ _ _ ⊖ _ _ _
7. _ _ _ ⊖ _ _
8. _ _ ⊖ _
9. _ _ _ ⊖ _

Such a wind was worth the wait.

⊖ ⊖ ⊖ ⊖ ⊖ ⊖ ⊖ ⊖ ⊖

(Acts 2:1–2)

151

Eternal Life

1. ANRE
2. EGNER
3. EIGES
4. SRRUEL
5. SGERLID
6. ESRITS
7. NDOEIRSI
8. NCOIANT
9. RSECATT
10. TPIY
11. UHSOE
12. NAEHEHT

1. _ _ _ Ⓞ
2. _ _ Ⓞ _ _
3. Ⓞ _ _ _ _
4. _ Ⓞ _ _ _ _
5. _ _ Ⓞ _ _ _ _
6. _ _ _ _ Ⓞ
7. _ Ⓞ _ _ _ _ _ _
8. Ⓞ _ _ _ _ _
9. _ _ _ _ Ⓞ _ _
10. _ Ⓞ _ _
11. _ Ⓞ _ _ _
12. _ _ _ _ _ _ Ⓞ

What is it that all believers will experience?

Ⓞ Ⓞ Ⓞ Ⓞ Ⓞ Ⓞ Ⓞ Ⓞ Ⓞ Ⓞ Ⓞ Ⓞ

(Acts 17:31–32)

152

Anointing

---

1. **DLEBSES**
2. **RIPSIT**
3. **UNORM**
4. **DFAOBRE**
5. **LPEINCAN**

1. _ _ _ ⊖ _ _ _
2. _ _ ⊖ _ _ _
3. ⊖ _ _ _ _
4. _ ⊖ _ _ _ _ _
5. _ _ _ ⊖ _ _ _ _

He threw a party for Jesus but was not prepared
for the woman with the perfume.

(Mark 14:3)

Tots

1. LREEVI
2. EGAELIL
3. ETLEPM
4. YCROTUN
5. ELNGA
6. DEHRA

7. ERCOJIE
8. DROHE
9. NROPSI
10. ELRPA
11. DBEAL

1. __ __ __ __ Ⓞ __
2. __ __ __ Ⓞ __ __ __
3. Ⓞ __ __ __ __ __
4. __ __ __ Ⓞ __ __
5. __ __ __ __ Ⓞ
6. __ Ⓞ __ __ __
7. __ __ __ __ __ Ⓞ __
8. Ⓞ __ __ __ __
9. __ __ Ⓞ __ __ __
10. __ __ __ __ Ⓞ
11. __ __ __ Ⓞ __

Who is like the greatest in heaven?

Ⓞ Ⓞ Ⓞ Ⓞ Ⓞ Ⓞ   Ⓞ Ⓞ Ⓞ Ⓞ Ⓞ

(Matthew 19:14)

154

Tumbling Walls

1. SJEUS
2. SDLEMA
3. RDPEAT
4. MITE
5. ECVIEER
6. HRONO
7. MKOIDNG

1. ⊖ _ _ _ _
2. _ _ _ _ ⊖ _
3. _ _ _ _ ⊖ _
4. _ ⊖ _ _
5. _ _ ⊖ _ _ _ _
6. ⊖ _ _ _ _
7. _ _ _ _ ⊖ _

Many feet meant a dramatic change for this place.

(Joshua 6)

A Fragrant Blend

1. LADISE
2. RNTAUE
3. HSTLO
4. GNVEI
5. ASRNE
6. ENCTOMPT
7. ENITATR
8. RCIPEN
9. AGSRS

1. _ ⊖ _ _ _ _
2. ⊖ _ _ _ _ _
3. _ _ ⊖ _ _ _
4. _ ⊖ _ _ _
5. _ ⊖ _ _ _
6. _ _ _ ⊖ _ _ _ _
7. ⊖ _ _ _ _ _ _
8. _ _ _ ⊖ _ _
9. ⊖ _ _ _ _

Many who had a important job to do for the Lord received this first. What was it?

◯◯◯◯◯◯◯◯

(Exodus 29:7)

156

Flour and Oil

1. DZINO
2. TBATEL
3. SRINIG
4. BSTERI
5. SPILNA

6. STHTRNEG
7. TCSHOAIR
8. WTODRA
9. EHTDA

1. ⊖ _ _ _ _
2. _ ⊖ _ _ _ _
3. ⊖ _ _ _ _ _
4. _ _ _ _ ⊖ _
5. ⊖ _ _ _ _
6. _ _ _ _ _ _ ⊖
7. _ _ ⊖ _ _ _ _
8. ⊖ _ _ _ _ _
9. _ _ _ _ ⊖

This town was home to a widow and her son who were very glad to have Elijah stay with them.

⊖⊖⊖⊖⊖⊖⊖⊖⊖

(1 Kings 17:9)

Glory of God

1. VAEBO
2. CZRACU
3. TUJNEDGM
4. AWONMRK
5. NIWGILL
6. CEESRIV
7. LBOSW

1. __ __ __ __ Ⓞ

2. Ⓞ __ __ __ __ __

3. __ __ __ __ __ Ⓞ __ __

4. __ __ __ Ⓞ __ __ __

5. __ Ⓞ __ __ __ __ __

6. __ __ __ __ __ __ Ⓞ

7. __ __ __ Ⓞ __

Wheels and scrolls—a vision for this prophet.
Who was he?

Ⓞ Ⓞ Ⓞ Ⓞ Ⓞ Ⓞ Ⓞ

(Ezekiel 1)

Out of the Water

1. **OBJ**
2. **EADPPTNOI**
3. **PRSTOO**
4. **SRERTOR**
5. **RISPLAL**
6. **EBDZEE**
7. **TEDXAEL**

1. _ _ ⊖
2. ⊖ _ _ _ _ _ _ _ _
3. _ _ _ _ ⊖ _
4. ⊖ _ _ _ _ _ _
5. _ ⊖ _ _ _ _
6. ⊖ _ _ _ _ _
7. _ _ _ _ _ ⊖ _

In the old days, a little water would clean one right up!

⊖ ⊖ ⊖ ⊖ ⊖ ⊖ ⊖

(Matthew 3:6)

159

Separation

1. SOECMNU
2. LEXTA
3. AEPELRUS
4. NSTERAV
5. EANRWS
6. RHIOPWS
7. RAUPETS

1. _ _ _ _ _ _ ◯
2. _ ◯ _ _ _
3. ◯ _ _ _ _ _ _ _
4. _ _ _ _ ◯ _ _
5. _ ◯ _ _ _ _
6. _ _ _ ◯ _ _ _
7. _ _ _ _ _ _ ◯

In the beginning, there was nothing to separate the water until God created it. What was it?

(Genesis 1:6)

Fear vs. Faith

1. NAEET
2. EBSON
3. ETLEBRIR
4. RHTHAE
5. SRUIOGEHT
6. EOCRNDAIN
7. YEMEN

1. _ ⊖ _ _ _
2. ⊖ _ _ _ _
3. _ _ ⊖ _ _ _ _ _
4. _ _ ⊖ _ _ _
5. _ _ _ ⊖ _ _ _ _ _
6. _ _ _ _ _ ⊖ _ _ _
7. _ _ _ ⊖ _

This righteous man had a difficult time with fear.

○○○○○○○

(Genesis 20–22)

Land Inheritance

1. HJAEIRME
2. OTERULB
3. KSAPE
4. RNHEEIT
5. DBLUI
6. HTSAIRSH

1. Ⓞ _ _ _ _ _ _ _
2. _ _ Ⓞ _ _ _ _
3. Ⓞ _ _ _ _
4. _ _ _ _ Ⓞ _ _
5. _ Ⓞ _ _ _
6. _ Ⓞ _ _ _ _ _ _

This son of Nun took control of a nation.

Ⓞ Ⓞ Ⓞ Ⓞ Ⓞ Ⓞ

(Numbers 34:17)

Barley Harvest

1. **SWSIELNDRE**
2. **YCROTUN**
3. **TWHAE**
4. **TWHEGI**
5. **RMEREMEB**
6. **RLDO**
7. **EBTRALEC**
8. **OZNI**

1. __ __ __ __ __ (O) __ __ __ __

2. __ (O) __ __ __ __

3. __ __ __ (O)

4. __ __ __ __ (O) __

5. __ __ __ __ __ (O) __ __

6. __ (O) __ __

7. __ __ (O) __ __ __

8. (O) __ __ __

This couple fell in love on a threshing floor.

(O)(O)(O)(O) and (O)(O)(O)(O)

(Ruth 2)

From Gath

1. **AGTRE**
2. **EHOSSR**
3. **SLJUEOA**
4. **DTIMS**
5. **MJEELRAUS**
6. **TPELMUM**
7. **SHTOS**

1. ◯ _ _ _ _
2. _ ◯ _ _ _ _
3. _ _ _ ◯ _ _ _
4. _ ◯ _ _ _
5. _ _ _ _ ◯ _ _ _
6. _ _ _ _ _ _ ◯
7. ◯ _ _ _ _

He should have ducked. Who was he?

◯◯◯◯◯◯

(1 Samuel 17:49)

No Darkness

1. LSUIFN
2. RFEAHT
3. EALSBSEM
4. NVOISI
5. SGSLEAND

6. NBERHETR
7. HFTAI
8. DOEPEN
9. DFNOU

1. ○ _ _ _ _ _
2. _ ○ _ _ _ _
3. _ _ _ _ _ _ ○ _
4. ○ _ _ _ _
5. _ _ ○ _ _ _ _ _
6. _ _ _ ○ _ _ _ _
7. _ _ ○ _ _
8. ○ _ _ _ _ _
9. _ _ _ ○ _

Whom shall we fear when the Lord is our light and our. . .?

○○○○○○○○○

(Psalm 27:1)

165

Blessing of Wisdom

1. **ASIMAAR**
2. **ERVEMO**
3. **ESEPRHUCL**
4. **DAENTION**
5. **MBETEHLHE**
6. **TCNOAVNE**
7. **NCIAATP**

1. Ⓞ _ _ _ _ _ _
2. _ _ _ Ⓞ _ _
3. _ _ _ _ Ⓞ _ _ _ _
4. _ _ Ⓞ _ _ _ _
5. _ _ _ _ _ _ _ _ Ⓞ
6. _ Ⓞ _ _ _ _ _ _
7. _ _ _ _ _ _ Ⓞ

He made the right choice and was blessed more than any other man.

(1 Kings 3)

Secrets of a Queen

1. **RDEEVLI**
2. **EPCRENES**
3. **NCIEART**
4. **NHEEVA**
5. **SFDIEL**
6. **EPSRIA**

1. _ Ⓞ _ _ _ _ _
2. _ _ _ Ⓞ _ _ _ _
3. _ _ _ Ⓞ _ _ _
4. Ⓞ _ _ _ _ _
5. _ _ Ⓞ _ _ _
6. _ Ⓞ _ _ _ _

She became queen and saved Israel. Who was she?

Ⓞ Ⓞ Ⓞ Ⓞ Ⓞ Ⓞ

(Esther 2:22–23)

Timeless Teaching

1. TLNAEM
2. ESCEIRV
3. ECMO
4. DBLEOH
5. YTTWNE
6. EFKOARS

7. DBLIU
8. TDREPA
9. LSUO
10. EHATS
11. EVYALL
12. SESTRNVA

1. _ _ _ Ⓞ _ _

2. _ _ _ _ _ Ⓞ _

3. Ⓞ _ _ _

4. _ _ _ _ Ⓞ _

5. _ _ Ⓞ _ _ _

6. _ _ _ Ⓞ _ _ _

7. _ _ Ⓞ _ _

8. _ _ _ Ⓞ _ _

9. Ⓞ _ _ _

10. _ _ _ Ⓞ _

11. _ _ _ _ Ⓞ _

12. _ _ _ _ _ _ _ Ⓞ

This book of the Bible is good for learning.

Ⓞ Ⓞ Ⓞ Ⓞ Ⓞ Ⓞ Ⓞ Ⓞ Ⓞ Ⓞ Ⓞ

A Governor's Decision

1. **RPEOTR**
2. **SWSIETN**
3. **EDLIPSIC**
4. **DSEAV**
5. **RFEAHT**
6. **RSETGRNA**

1. ◯ _ _ _ _ _
2. _ ◯ _ _ _ _ _
3. _ _ _ _ _ ◯ _
4. _ ◯ _ _ _
5. _ _ ◯ _ _ _
6. _ _ _ _ _ _ ◯ _

He asked Jesus if He was the King of the Jews.

◯◯◯◯◯◯

(Matthew 27:11)

The Prophetess

1. **DUEDHRN**
2. **SREET**
3. **UHECIBMR**
4. **SHUEO**
5. **NRDGUO**
6. **RESMSAUE**
7. **AHRCSE**

1. _ _ _ _ _ _ Ⓞ
2. _ _ Ⓞ _ _
3. _ _ _ _ _ Ⓞ _ _
4. _ Ⓞ _ _ _
5. _ Ⓞ _ _ _ _
6. _ _ Ⓞ _ _ _ _ _
7. _ _ _ Ⓞ _ _

She was a female judge who ruled Israel.

(Judges 4:4)

Puffed Up?

1. KTNHI
2. SNANOTI
3. WRGO
4. SPSWAORR
5. SLIELI

6. SRNAEV
7. YEDLA
8. SGERVA
9. SCSERBI

1. _ _ _ _ Ⓞ
2. Ⓞ _ _ _ _ _ _
3. _ _ Ⓞ _
4. _ _ _ _ _ _ Ⓞ _
5. _ _ Ⓞ _ _ _
6. _ _ _ Ⓞ _ _
7. Ⓞ _ _ _ _
8. Ⓞ _ _ _ _ _
9. _ _ _ _ _ Ⓞ _

Charity edifies, but this puffs up. What is it?

Ⓞ Ⓞ Ⓞ Ⓞ Ⓞ Ⓞ Ⓞ Ⓞ

(1 Corinthians 8:1)

Obeying the Truth

1. YGLRO
2. RMEANN
3. KWLA
4. EALNG
5. TPERAIV

6. ERSPIOM
7. YGIRANP
8. TANCUCO
9. EPSLAE

1. ◯ _ _ _ _
2. _ ◯ _ _ _ _
3. _ _ ◯ _
4. ◯ _ _ _ _
5. _ _ _ _ _ ◯ _
6. _ _ _ _ ◯ _ _
7. _ _ ◯ _ _ _ _
8. _ _ _ _ ◯ _
9. _ _ _ _ ◯ _

Who were these people who were bewitched?

◯◯◯◯◯◯◯◯◯

(Galatians 3:1)

172

Disciples

1. RTNEE
2. HISTTE
3. TINFSIRMIEI
4. RCDNIETO

5. EOTMRH
6. LHYO
7. RFTOY

1. _ _ Ⓞ _ _

2. _ Ⓞ _ _ _ _

3. _ _ _ _ Ⓞ _ _ _ _ _

4. _ Ⓞ _ _ _ _ _ _

5. _ _ Ⓞ _ _ _

6. Ⓞ _ _ _

7. _ _ _ _ Ⓞ

Who was Paul's own son in the faith?

Ⓞ Ⓞ Ⓞ Ⓞ Ⓞ Ⓞ Ⓞ

(1 Corinthians 4:17)

The Wicked Revealed

1. EHLFS
2. RLBIYTE
3. NIRTTWE
4. RNEUD
5. AECRG
6. TBDWSEOE
7. LARGYLOE
8. AINSI
9. AOGDNBE
10. VLAENE
11. RTHSIC
12. SOANSE

1. _ Ⓞ _ _ _
2. _ _ _ _ _ _ Ⓞ
3. _ _ Ⓞ _ _ _ _
4. _ Ⓞ _ _ _
5. Ⓞ _ _ _ _
6. _ _ _ _ _ Ⓞ
7. _ _ _ _ _ Ⓞ _ _
8. _ _ Ⓞ _ _
9. _ _ Ⓞ _ _ _
10. _ Ⓞ _ _ _
11. _ _ Ⓞ _ _ _
12. Ⓞ _ _ _ _ _

Satan comes with all power, signs, and what else?

Ⓞ Ⓞ Ⓞ Ⓞ Ⓞ   Ⓞ Ⓞ Ⓞ Ⓞ Ⓞ Ⓞ

(2 Thessalonians 2:9)

Fair Pay

1. ETGHNSRT
2. NIONOMDI
3. TASSNI
4. TRABHED
5. WROEP

6. USWHLIF
7. HARETG
8. TWRHA
9. NURPCDEE

1. _ _ _ _ _ _ _ Ⓞ
2. _ _ _ Ⓞ _ _ _ _
3. Ⓞ _ _ _ _ _
4. _ Ⓞ _ _ _ _ _
5. _ _ _ Ⓞ _
6. Ⓞ _ _ _ _ _ _
7. _ Ⓞ _ _ _ _
8. _ Ⓞ _ _ _
9. _ _ _ Ⓞ _ _ _ _

What is a laborer worthy of?

Ⓞ Ⓞ Ⓞ Ⓞ Ⓞ Ⓞ Ⓞ Ⓞ

(1 Corinthians 3:8)

175

Answers

7
1. EMBRACE
2. WISDOM
3. KNOWLEDGE
4. ESTEEM
5. SPIRIT
6. SIGHT
7. YEARS
8. PRESENT
9. DEPTH
10. PLACE

Keeping God's commands will prolong your life and bring PROSPERITY.

8
1. VIPERS
2. SALTINESS
3. BROTHER
4. TRAMPLE
5. HEAVEN
6. DESERT
7. WARNING
8. FREEZE

It was a new home after Egypt.
NAZARETH

9
1. JUDGE
2. DARKNESS
3. NARROW
4. REWARDS
5. ADVERSARY
6. FASTING
7. LEGAL
8. OFFICER

Once this is lost, it's not good for anything.
SALTINESS

10
1. PROCLAIM
2. JAILER
3. PROVINCE
4. INHABIT
5. CUSTOM
6. UPROAR
7. TRAVEL
8. FLEET
9. CAREFUL

"When they had passed through Amphipolis and APOLLONIA they came to Thessalonica, where there was a Jewish synagogue."

11
1. CRUCIFIED
2. FAITH
3. ETERNAL
4. NATURE
5. INCREASE
6. BAPTISM
7. CONTROL
8. WAGES

Death is the release from
MARRIAGE.

12
1. RANSOM
2. OVERTHROW
3. REBUKE
4. RESPECT
5. WICKEDNESS
6. PRUDENT

A MOCKER never listens to instruction or advice.

13
1. GENEROUS
2. PROPORTION
3. ENCOURAGE
4. BROKEN
5. DISOBEDIENT
6. ACCORD
7. HIMSELF

This is left by God's choice.
REMNANT

14
1. DESCENDANT
2. PASSAGE
3. ASCEND
4. GRAFTED
5. CHEERFUL
6. JOSEPH
7. GOVERN
8. MOUTH

Think of yourself with sober JUDGMENT.

15
1. CONSIDER
2. ACCEPT
3. GLORIFY
4. MATERIAL
5. SAINTS
6. SCRIPTURE
7. REMAIN
8. PRAISE
9. CONDEMN

May the God who gives "ENDURANCE and encouragement give you a spirit of unity among yourselves as you follow Christ Jesus."

16
1. EXILED
2. HISTORIC
3. ANSWER
4. REQUEST
5. REBUILD
6. DEDICATE
7. CALVARY
8. REPAIR

They became BUILDERS to fulfill Nehemiah's vision.

17

1. S E R V A N T
2. T H O U S A N D
3. B O R D E R
4. J U D A H
5. S H I N I N G
6. M O A B I T E
7. P O R T I O N
8. P R O S P E R

"The wife of a man from the company of the P R O P H E T S cried out to Elisha, 'Your servant my husband is dead, and you know that he revered the LORD. But now his creditor is coming to take my two boys as his slaves.' "

18

1. P I L L A R
2. G U I D E
3. A B A N D O N
4. E N J O Y
5. H A R D S H I P
6. E X A L T E D
7. H A N D F U L
8. T H O U G H T

"The J E S H A N A H Gate was repaired by Joiada son of Paseah and Meshullam son of Besodeiah."

19

1. N E G L E C T
2. M A R R I A G E
3. N E H E M I A H
4. S P E A K
5. S O L O M O N
6. F O R E I G N
7. H O U S E H O L D
8. A C C O U N T
9. A C C O R D
10. G R A I N

It was here that Eliashib the priest had been put in charge in the house of God. S T O R E R O O M S

20

1. S T A N D I N G
2. C O V E N A N T
3. J O S H U A
4. T H O U S A N D
5. W A T E R
6. S T O N E S
7. D I R E C T
8. F U L F I L L E D
9. J O R D A N
10. M O N T H

" 'Be strong and courageous, because you will lead these people to inherit the land I swore to their F O R E F A T H E R S to give them.' "

21

1. R I C H E S
2. P R O S P E R I T Y
3. C H A S I N G
4. T O I L I N G
5. B E N E F I T
6. S H E L T E R
7. P R E S E R V E
8. E X T R E M E

"All man's efforts are for his mouth, yet his A P P E T I T E is never satisfied."

22

1. T E R R I T O R Y
2. N O R T H
3. O C C U P Y
4. S T R O N G E R
5. P E O P L E
6. T O W N
7. R E S I D E
8. B E L O N G
9. E A S T E R N
10. I S R A E L

A place of refuge was provided for those guilty of this. U N I N T E N T I O N A L killing

23

1. D O O R
2. S O U T H E R N
3. C R A V E D
4. D I S T R E S S
5. S T R E A M S
6. C H A R I O T
7. W H I R L W I N D
8. C L O U D
9. B E L I E V E
10. E N O U G H

"Men ate the B R E A D of A N G E L S; he sent them all the food they could eat."

24

1. E X A L T E D
2. R E J O I C E
3. P O W E R
4. R E N O U N C E
5. F O U N D
6. M O R N I N G
7. A N G R Y
8. R E D U C E
9. T H R O N E
10. E N E M I E S

Righteousness and justice are the F O U N D A T I O N of God's throne.

25

1. B R O N Z E
2. S H O W E R S
3. D E S T I N E D
4. R E P R O A C H
5. S U F F E R
6. A P P O I N T
7. D R I V E N
8. T O U C H
9. F I G H T
10. R E S C U E

"You understand, O LORD; remember me and care for me. Avenge me on my P E R S E C U T O R S."

26

1. I G N O R A N T
2. B E C A U S E
3. P L O W M A N
4. C R O W N
5. A P O S T L E
6. R E V E L R Y
7. T H A N K S G I V I N G
8. T E M P T E D
9. L I V I N G

The man who *thinks* he knows something believes he has this. K N O W L E D G E

177

27

1. S U R V (I) V O R
2. S H (E) P H E R D S
3. P (E) A C E F U L
4. W R A T (H)
5. (M) E A D O W S
6. B U (R) I E D
7. (J) U S T I C E
8. T R E (A) D

To (J)(E)(R)(E)(M)(I)(A)(H), the Lord spoke that the nations would drink from the cup of wrath.

28

1. M E R C H A N (T)
2. C (E) D A R
3. B A N (N) E R
4. S (P) O K E N
5. H O R R (I) B L E
6. R E (N) O W N
7. P (U) N I S H
8. C A (M) E L
9. (S) T R E T C H
10. (H) O S T I L E

There was a prophecy of (P)(U)(N)(I)(S)(H)(M)(E)(N)(T) against Moab.

29

1. (S) U B M I T
2. F (O) R M E R
3. C H U R C (H)
4. C (O) R N E R S T O N E
5. S E R V I C (E)
6. U N I T E (D)
7. S (L) A N D E R
8. (F) O O L I S H
9. B L (A) M E L E S S

"Therefore each of you must put off (F)(A)(L)(S)(E)(H)(O)(O)(D) and speak truthfully to his neighbor, for we are all members of one body."

30

1. T R A N S - G R E S S I O N (S)
2. R E (A) L M S
3. K I N (D) N E S S
4. (C) R E A T E
5. A D V A (N) C E
6. R U L (E) R
7. (D) O M I N I O N
8. E P H (E) S U S

Up, up, and away! (A)(S)(C)(E)(N)(D)(E)(D)

31

1. E L D (E) R
2. A C C O (U) N T
3. (S) U R P R I S E D
4. M I (D) D L E
5. S T E A D (F) A S T
6. (R) E G A R D
7. P R E A C H (E) D
8. (F) R E E D O M

Done with sin: (S)(U)(F)(F)(E)(R)(E)(D) in the body

32

1. M A R R (I) A G E
2. (U) N I T E D
3. C O V E T (I) N G
4. D E S I R E (S)
5. S L A V (E)
6. F A I (T) H
7. (H) U M A N
8. J E S U (S)
9. B (O) U N D
10. L O (N) G E R
11. C H (R) I S T
12. E T (E) R N A L

We have eternal life in Christ as grace reigns through (R)(I)(G)(H)(T)(E)(O)(U)(S)(N)(E)(S)(S)

33

1. (P) U R I F I E D
2. (S) H I E L D
3. E N D U R (I) N G
4. W I T H E (R) S
5. M (O) U R N
6. O B E (Y)
7. S A N (C) T I F Y
8. E M P T (Y)
9. B L E M I S (H)

"Therefore, rid yourselves of all malice and all deceit, (H)(Y)(P)(O)(C)(R)(I)(S)(Y), envy, and slander of every kind."

34

1. (A) N C E S T O R
2. I M P A R T (I) A L
3. S U B (M) I T
4. H U M (B) L E
5. H A R B (O) R
6. S E L F (I) S H
7. S I (N) C E R E
8. C O N V I C (T)

"But if you harbor bitter envy and selfish (A)(M)(B)(I)(T)(I)(O)(N) in your hearts, do not boast about it or deny the truth."

35

1. S H U D (D) E R
2. (M) I R R O R
3. C O R (R) U P T
4. T A M (E)
5. R (O) Y A L
6. (E) X P L O I T
7. (F) A D I N G

Look into the perfect law and receive (F)(R)(E)(E)(D)(O)(M).

36

1. C H (I) L D H O O D
2. C E R T I F I C A T (E)
3. E N V E L O P (E)
4. T O G E T H E (R)
5. A R G U (E)
6. B E T R (A) Y E D
7. L A W F U (L)
8. R E B U K (E)
9. G O D L I N E S (S)
10. A G A I N S (T)

To make as white as the light. (T)(R)(A)(N)(S)(F)(I)(G)(U)(R)(E)

178

37

1. NATIONS
2. CONDEMNED
3. AUTHORITY
4. LANGUAGES
5. VIOLENCE
6. BLESSED
7. ROBE

Smoke will rise high from this place.
BABYLON

38

1. STRIKE
2. DELIVER
3. DEBTORS
4. MEASURE
5. WORRY
6. BORROW
7. FORGIVE
8. PIECES
9. UNDER

"'Watch out for false prophets. They come to you in sheep's clothing, but inwardly they are FEROCIOUS wolves.'"

39

1. SORROW
2. IMAGINE
3. BOUND
4. WITNESS
5. LINGER
6. DRUNKARD
7. FOLLY

A narrow well is this wife.
WAYWARD

40

1. WICKED
2. WATER
3. REFLECT
4. SILVER
5. MALICE
6. SUDDEN
7. NOTHING
8. GREEDY
9. SHARPEN
10. INCENSE

"Anger is cruel and fury OVERWHELMING, but who can stand before jealousy?"

41

1. MORNING
2. MEANINGLESS
3. DANGER
4. REMEMBER
5. HIDDEN
6. BLESSED
7. AFTERWARD
8. MADNESS

"The words of the wise are like goads, their collected sayings like firmly EMBEDDED nails—given by one Shepherd."

42

1. DEFILE
2. CONSUME
3. OPPRESS
4. NUMBER
5. SWORE
6. SNARE
7. CREDIT
8. CUSTOMS
9. FAMINE
10. HANDS

"Therefore the LORD was angry with his people and abhorred his INHERITANCE."

43

1. DECEPTION
2. PROTECT
3. WICKED
4. VAIN
5. FURNACE
6. JUSTICE
7. NATIONS
8. HEART

Where are the godly? The faithful have VANISHED.

44

1. WOMAN
2. BABYLON
3. BREASTPLATE
4. TEMPLE
5. MANKIND
6. ALTAR
7. STOMACH
8. DESTROY
9. TORRENT

"Now when they have finished their TESTIMONY, the beast that comes up from the Abyss will attack them, and overpower and kill them."

45

1. CURTAIN
2. CEREMONY
3. UNCLEAN
4. EVENING
5. BURNED
6. OFFERING
7. BATHE
8. BLOOD

Don't eat this!
FORBIDDEN blood

46

1. CONSECRATE
2. ACCEPT
3. DEFECT
4. VALUE
5. MARRIAGE
6. FILTHY
7. ALLOW
8. PROFANE
9. LORD
10. TOUCH

"When anyone brings from the herd or flock a FELLOWSHIP offering to the LORD to fulfill a special vow or as a freewill offering, it must be without defect or blemish to be acceptable."

47

1. W O M A (N)
2. C (O) N F E S S
3. D (I) R E C T (I) O N
4. (S) A C R E D
5. E N T R A N C (E)
6. A R T (I) C L E (S)
7. R E L A T (I) V E
8. (G) O L D
9. S E R V E
10. T E N T (H)

These clans carried the curtains for the tabernacle, the tent of meeting.
(G E R S H O N I T E S)

48

1. L I V E (S) T O C K
2. B R (O) N Z E
3. J O (U) R N E Y
4. T R A V E (L)
5. (M) E S S E N G E R
6. D E S T R (O) Y
7. V I (O) L A T E
8. D E (N) I E D

When the Israelites spoke against the Lord and Moses, (V E N O M O U S) snakes were sent among them.

49

1. P H I L I S T (I) N E
2. D I S G (R) A C E
3. (S) E R V A N T
4. D A (V) I D
5. D E L I V (E) R
6. S A M U (E) L
7. T U N I (C)

David came to Saul and entered his
"(S E R V I C E). Saul liked him very much, and David became one of his armor-bearers."

50

1. H E B R (O) N
2. (J) E B U S I T E
3. A M O I N (T)
4. (F) E A S T
5. L A W L E S (S)
6. O F F S P R I N G
7. H (O) U S E
8. P R O M I (S) E

David captured the
(F O R T R E S S) of Zion and would call it the City of David.

51

1. H U (M) I L I T Y
2. A C C (O) M P A N I E D
3. G R A P E V I N E
4. P R O (D) U C E
5. (S) P R I N G
6. (W) O R T H L E S S

Two sides of true (W I S D O M).

52

1. R E F (U) S E
2. D I S G R A C (E)
3. (H) I T T I T E
4. B I R T (H) P L A C E
5. A N O I N T E (D)
6. M I L L S T O N E
7. G R (O) U N D
8. A R R (O) W
9. D E (S) O L A T E

"This is what the LORD says: 'Out of your own
(H O U S E H O L D) I am going to bring calamity upon you.'"

53

1. T W E L F (T) H
2. H (A) M A N
3. K I N G D O M
4. S (U) M M O N
5. P L E A S (E) D
6. N O (B) L E
7. O F F I C E R
8. G (U) A R D E D

King Xerxes was looking for a
(B E A U T I F U L) young wife.

54

1. P E R S I (A)
2. W (E) L F A R E
3. P E O P L (E)
4. A (C) C O U N T
5. B E T T (E) R
6. C O N T I (N) U E
7. M O R D E C A I
8. F A M I (L) Y
9. R E L (I) E F
10. C O (U) R I E R

"So the Jews agreed to continue the
(C E L E B R A T I O N) they had begun, doing what Mordecai had written to them."

55

1. (W) O N D E R S
2. M I (R) A C L E
3. U P W A R (D)
4. M (O) R T A L
5. H A R D S H I P
6. T U R M (O) I L
7. (N) I G H T
8. I N T E (G) R I T Y
9. (G) L I D E D
10. C O U (N) T

"In all this, Job did not sin by charging God with
(W R O N G D O I N G)."

56

1. R E P E N T A N C E
2. (A) N G E R
3. P E A C (E)
4. M E S S (A) G E
5. O V E R T H R O W
6. (B) E N J A M I N
7. P R O M I S (E)
8. S A B B A T H

"When (B A R N A B A S) and Saul had finished their mission, they returned from Jerusalem, taking with them John, also called Mark."

57
1. P(I)LGRIMA(G)E
2. (A)LMIGHTY
3. STRE(N)GTH
4. FAV(O)R
5. PRI(N)CE
6. SUB(D)UE
7. (B)ESTOW
8. TRUST

"You are forgiving and good, O Lord, (A)(B)(O)(U)(N)(D)(I)(N)(G) in love to all who call to you."

58
1. CREDI(T)OR
2. REMA(I)N
3. H(I)GH
4. WH(I)SPER
5. MEMOR(Y)
6. H(U)NGRY
7. (Q)UIETLY
8. (WO)NDERFUL

Of an evil man, may his (I)(N)(I)(Q)(U)(I)(T)(Y) be remembered before the Lord.

59
1. WILLIN(G)
2. (F)OOTSTEPS
3. RE(D)EEM
4. STAT(U)TE
5. P(U)NISH
6. C(O)NSIDER
7. SHI(E)LD
8. OPPRESSIO(N)

"The (U)(N)(F)(O)(L)(D)(I)(N)(G) of your words gives light; it gives understanding to the simple."

60
1. P(R)ECEPTS
2. PR(O)UD
3. WIC(K)ED
4. ANSWE(R)
5. (C)OURSE
6. SHUN(N)ED
7. PRUDEN(C)E
8. ABUNDAN(T)
9. M(O)UTH
10. UPR(I)GHT

Heed this, and you will have understanding. (C)(O)(R)(R)(E)(C)(T)(I)(O)(N)

61
1. C(O)NC(E)RN
2. GR(O)WTH
3. JUS(T)ICE
4. C(O)NCEAL
5. WIS(D)OM
6. BOAS(T)
7. (B)LAME(L)ESS
8. PRO(S)PER
9. DEAF
10. PRA(Y)ER

"(B)(L)(O)(O)(D)(T)(H)(I)(R)(S)(T)(Y) men hate a man of integrity and seek to kill the upright."

62
1. NUM(B)ER
2. V(I)SION
3. MY(R)TLE
4. S(H)AKE
5. R(A)ISED
6. MEA(S)URE
7. ES(C)APE
8. BAPTI(Z)E
9. S(H)OUT

This king's name is hard to spell. (Z)(E)(C)(H)(A)(R)(I)(A)(H)

63
1. (D)REA(D)FUL
2. PRES(E)RVE
3. (S)PARE
4. DE(C)REES
5. PRO(S)PER
6. H(E)ALING
7. W(I)NGS
8. (T)RAMPLE
9. H(A)RSH
10. E(N)OUGH

" 'I the LORD do not change. So you, O (D)(E)(S)(C)(E)(N)(D)(A)(N)(T)(S) of Jacob, are not destroyed.' "

64
1. L(A)B(A)N
2. STRE(N)GT(H)
3. F(A)T(H)ER
4. (R)A(C)HEL
5. A(N)IMALS
6. TR(O)UGH(S)
7. (D)E(C)EIT
8. (S)EVE(N)
9. IN(H)ERI(T)
10. GILE(A)(D)
11. BRAN(C)H(E)S

Laban kissed his (G)(R)(A)(N)(D)(C)(H)(I)(L)(D)(R)(E)(N) and daughters good-bye.

65
1. FAV(O)(R)
2. AFFLICTE(D)
3. (R)EVOKED
4. HORSEME(N)
5. PASTUR(E)
6. SLAUGHT(E)R

" 'These are the things you are to do: Speak the truth to each other, and (R)(E)(N)(D)(E)(R) true and sound judgment in your courts.' "

66
1. (B)LOODY
2. (B)URNING
3. BLOODS(H)ED
4. TOLER(A)TE
5. (K)NOWLEDGE
6. WOODWOR(K)
7. ORD(A)IN
8. DRUN(K)ARD

Another hard name to spell. (H)(A)(B)(A)(K)(K)(U)(K)

67

1. S T O N E S
2. L A B O R
3. E X H A U S T
4. I N C R E A S E
5. C O M P L A I N T
6. T R E A C H E R Y
7. S C O F F
8. L O C U S T S
9. F O R T R E S S
10. F I G

"You have plotted the ruin of many peoples, shaming your own house and F O R F E I T I N G your life."

68

1. B O N E S
2. P R O T E C T
3. S A L V A T I O N
4. V I N D I C A T E
5. D W E L L
6. P I E R C E D
7. U P H O L D
8. S U S T A I N
9. R E C O U N T

"I say to God my Rock, 'Why have you forgotten me? Why must I go about mourning, O P P R E S S E D by the enemy?' "

69

1. L A G G I N G
2. P O S S E S S
3. P R A I S E
4. A C Q U I T
5. T R E A T
6. A L T A R
7. C O M M A N D
8. D E T E S T
9. S O U L
10. M A R R Y

Old Testament book of the Bible. D E U T E R O N O M Y

70

1. A M O R I T E S
2. R E N E W A L
3. F O R S A K E
4. T R A C T
5. R E P O R T
6. B U R N T
7. B U R I E D
8. D E S I R A B L E
9. H U M I L I T Y
10. C O U N T R Y

"Then Joshua sent the people away, each to his own I N H E R I T A N C E."

71

1. D E A T H
2. H I M S E L F
3. L E A V E
4. F O R T U N E
5. W R O T E
6. R E A D I N G
7. C O U R A G E
8. A F R A I D
9. G A T H E R
10. I S A A C

"See, I set before you today life and prosperity, death and D E S T R U C T I O N."

72

1. E L D E R L Y
2. L E N G T H
3. D E C E I V E
4. H O N E S T
5. Q U A N T I T I E S
6. S T A N D A R D
7. F O R G I V E
8. D I V I N E
9. C A S T

" 'Observe my Sabbaths and have R E V E R E N C E for my sanctuary. I am the LORD.' "

73

1. R E B E K A H
2. B E T H U E L
3. M A S T E R
4. S U C C E S S
5. C A M E L S
6. B R A C E L E T S
7. I S H M A E L

Another wife for Abraham. K E T U R A H

74

1. F R U I T
2. R E S P E C T
3. A L I E N S
4. A P P R O A C H
5. D I S H O N O R
6. T A T T O O
7. I M P U R E
8. M E E T I N G
9. G U I L T
10. V I N E Y A R D

" 'Do not turn to mediums or seek out S P I R I T I S T S, for you will be defiled by them. I am the LORD your God.' "

75

1. I N F E C T
2. S E V E N T H
3. S W E L L I N G
4. S H A V E D
5. P R O N O U N C E
6. E X A M I N E
7. C L O T H E S
8. M U S T Y

A place of worship. S A N C T U A R Y

76

1. F L E S H
2. D I S E A S E
3. Y E L L O W
4. B E G I N
5. F A D E D
6. P R I E S T
7. I S O L A T E
8. C R E A T U R E
9. P R E G N A N T
10. D E L A Y

" 'Every creature that moves about on the ground is D E T E S T A B L E; it is not to be eaten.' "

182

77

1. J A C O B
2. C A R E F U L
3. D I V I N A T I O N
4. C H I L D R E N
5. M A I D E N S
6. S P E C K L E D
7. T R O U G H

Set up a tent.
P I T C H E D

78

1. N O T I C E D
2. L A B A N
3. F L O C K S
4. H O U S E H O L D
5. B L E S S E D
6. S E R V A N T
7. M A N D R A K E
8. B R A N C H

"After Rachel gave birth to Joseph, Jacob said to Laban, 'Send me on my way so I can go back to my own H O M E L A N D.'"

79

1. B R E A D
2. D E A D E N E D
3. F A I T H
4. E X A M P L E
5. F O L L O W
6. G L O R I F Y
7. Q U I C K L Y

A method of travel.
W A L K I N G

80

1. F R U I T F U L
2. C L A N S
3. C O V E N A N T
4. G A R M E N T
5. C R E A T U R E
6. F L O O D
7. O F F E R I N G S
8. E S T A B L I S H
9. Y O U N G E S T

It was hard to get any work done with men speaking so many different
L A N G U A G E S

81

1. R E F U S E
2. A D V I S E D
3. C H A R G E
4. C R U C I F Y
5. L I S T E N I N G
6. T E M P L E
7. S C R I P T U R E
8. S A T I S F Y

One of prominent position.
P H A R I S E E

82

1. T R U M P E T
2. S O U N D E D
3. N U M B E R
4. T R I B E
5. G I G A N T I C
6. S C O R P I O N
7. F O R E H E A D
8. P O W E R
9. S M O K E
10. S T R I K E

Jesus said, "I am the
R E S U R R E C T I O N
and the life."

83

1. B A B Y L O N
2. M I L L S T O N E
3. C O N S U M E
4. B R I D E
5. R I D E R
6. M U L T I T U D E
7. A P O S T L E
8. T O R T U R E
9. C A R R I A G E
10. D O U B L E

" 'When you see Jerusalem being surrounded by armies, you will know that its
D E S O L A T I O N is near.' "

84

1. L O O P S
2. T A B E R N A C L E
3. L I N E N
4. C U B I T
5. K N O T
6. M O S E S
7. C O M M A N D

"All the S K I L L E D men among the workmen made the tabernacle with ten curtains of finely twisted linen and blue, purple and scarlet yarn, with cherubim worked into them by a skilled craftsman."

85

1. C L O A K
2. D E M A N D
3. M O R N I N G
4. M E R C I F U L
5. P H A R I S E E S
6. T A K E N
7. S A B B A T H
8. R E W A R D

"But a S A M A R I T A N, as he traveled, came where the man was; and when he saw him, he took pity on him."

86

1. P A R A B L E
2. S I N F U L
3. G A T H E R I N G
4. M O I S T U R E
5. T R A M P L E D
6. P R O V E N
7. B I R D S
8. A C C O U N T

One of the seven stars.
L A O D I C E A

87
1. M I G H T Y
2. P R O C L A I M
3. D A V I D
4. B E T H L E H E M
5. R I S K E D
6. S P E A R
7. D E F E N D
8. S T R O N G H O L D
9. G A R R I S O N
10. E X P L O I T S

The P H I L I S T I N E S
found Saul and his sons fallen on Mount Gilboa.

88
1. T H O U S A N D
2. F A L S E H O O D
3. O M E G A
4. C O N T I N U E
5. G L A S S
6. R E I G N E D
7. Y I E L D I N G
8. P L A G U E S
9. W I L L I N G

Two of them could shut up the sky.
W I T N E S S E S

89
1. R E V E R E N C E
2. S E R P E N T
3. D R A G O N
4. E U P H R A T E S
5. P E A L S
6. R U M B L I N G
7. I N J U R Y
8. D E M O N S

"They overcame him by the blood of the Lamb
and by the word of their
T E S T I M O N Y".

90
1. B L A S P H E M E
2. S C E P T E R
3. F A T A L
4. E X E R C I S E
5. F O U G H T
6. W R A T H
7. G I V E N

The time has come for the
H A R V E S T of the earth.

91
1. H A R P I S T
2. A N G E L
3. T R E M E N D O U S
4. F I L L E D
5. H A I L S T O N E S
6. K I N G S
7. R E V E A L
8. F O L L O W

Not a good place to be.
A R M A G E D D O N

92
1. P H A R A O H
2. B L I N D
3. W O R S H I P
4. C A N A A N
5. J U D G M E N T
6. M O U N T A I N
7. I S R A E L I T E
8. S A C R I F I C E
9. Q U O T A
10. S C A T T E R

"Then the LORD said, 'If they do not believe you or
pay attention to the first
M I R A C U L O U S sign, they
may believe the second.'"

93
1. R E C A L L E D
2. D E M A N D
3. A U T H O R I T Y
4. R A B B I
5. B U I L D
6. F O U N D
7. B R O U G H T
8. B E T H S A I D A
9. B E L I E V E
10. T E S T I M O N Y

A way of not speaking plainly.
F I G U R A T I V E
language

94
1. E T E R N A L
2. D I S C I P L E S
3. T I B E R I A S
4. M A N N A
5. U N L E S S
6. A M A Z I N G
7. A C C U S E R
8. G R U M B L E D
9. N O T H I N G
10. D E C L A R E

"Then came the Feast of
D E D I C A T I O N at
Jerusalem."

95
1. B E T H A N Y
2. D I N N E R
3. R E C L I N E
4. I S C A R I O T
5. S T U M B L E
6. Z E A L O U S
7. F R A G R A N C E

"Meanwhile a large crowd of Jews found out that
Jesus was there and came, not only because of
him but also to see L A Z A R U S,
whom he had raised from the dead."

96
1. S P L E N D O R
2. T R U S T
3. S E R V A N T
4. F A T H E R
5. O P P R E S S O R S
6. P R I D E
7. B E S T O W
8. P R E S E N C E
9. M E R C I F U L

"Praise be to the LORD, for he showed his
W O N D E R F U L love to me
when I was in a besieged city."

97

1. B O U N D
2. P U R P L E
3. P R O T E C T
4. O B J E C T E D
5. D E N I E D
6. R E B E L L I O N
7. P I L A T E

Seeing that which is ahead.
P R E D I C T

98

1. M I R A C L E
2. D R A G G E D
3. F I S H I N G
4. N I C O D E M U S
5. S O L D I E R
6. P E R M I S S I O N
7. G I V E N
8. P R E P A R E

Just before this, Jesus knew it was time to leave.
P A S S O V E R

99

1. A S T I R
2. I N D E E D
3. C R A D L E
4. H E A R T
5. M A R V E L O U S
6. D E V O T E D
7. F O R T H
8. F U R I O U S
9. P A S T U R E
10. R I G H T S

"Love and F A I T H F U L N E S S meet together; righteousness and peace kiss each other."

100

1. C H A R M E D
2. G R A C I O U S
3. B A T T L E
4. M U L T I P L I E S
5. M A D N E S S
6. S H A D O W
7. D E S E R V E

"If the ax is dull and its edge unsharpened, more strength is needed but skill will bring S U C C E S S."

101

1. C H A R I O T
2. G A T H E R
3. C O M P A S S I O N
4. F L A M E S
5. R E B U K E
6. P R A Y E R
7. B R E A T H
8. F O R E V E R
9. L O V E

He's really big and loves to frolic.
L E V I A T H A N

102

1. B R E A T H
2. U P W A R D
3. F R I E N D S
4. H A P P E N
5. E N J O Y M E N T
6. C O N T R O L
7. B E A U T I F U L
8. S I L E N T
9. D E S P A I R
10. C A V E R N

God made these to water groves of flourishing trees.
R E S E R V O I R S

103

1. J U D G M E N T
2. P R O J E C T S
3. F L O U R I S H
4. W I S D O M
5. B U R D E N
6. E N D U R E
7. R E V E R E
8. S T R A I G H T

"So I hated life, because the work that is done under the sun was G R I E V O U S to me. All of it is meaningless, a chasing after the wind."

104

1. L O V E R
2. V I N E Y A R D S
3. L E B A N O N
4. F L O W I N G
5. F O U N T A I N
6. J E W E L S
7. M O U N T A I N

He wrote a book of love.
S O L O M O N

105

1. H A N D L E S
2. C A P T I V E
3. T O W E R S
4. D E S C E N D
5. G R A C E F U L
6. W A I S T
7. C R A F T S M A N
8. M A J E S T I C

"The W A T C H M E N found me as they made their rounds in the city."

106

1. C O R N E R
2. N E I G H B O R
3. I N S T R U C T
4. C O R R U P T
5. R O O F T O P S
6. B E A T I N G
7. O V E R L O O K
8. Q U A R R E L

"P E N A L T I E S are prepared for mockers, and beatings for the backs of fools."

107

1. C O U N S E L O R
2. M A N K I N D
3. B A P T I Z E
4. J E R U S A L E M
5. E X A L T E D
6. D I S A S T E R
7. F A I T H F U L
8. T R E A S U R E
9. O F F I C I A L S
10. H O N O R

God spoke to I S A I A H son of A M O Z of what was to come.

108

1. I D L E N E S S
2. V I G O R
3. G A R M E N T S
4. S U R P A S S
5. T R E M B L E
6. C O N F I D E N C E
7. T R A D I N G
8. S W O R D S

"For as churning the milk produces butter, and as T W I S T I N G the nose produces blood, so stirring up anger produces strife."

109

1. F R I G H T E N
2. A N C I E N T
3. S A T R A P
4. I N S C R I B E
5. A T T E N D
6. P O W E R F U L
7. B O A S T F U L
8. A B L A Z E

In this deep and dark place could Daniel be found. L I O N S' D E N

110

1. C O N F E S S I O N
2. C O R P S E
3. C R I P P L E D
4. C E R T A I N
5. T E S T E D
6. S E P A R A T E
7. S U D D E N L Y
8. P E R S U A D E

They wondered why some people were so difficult to heal. D I S C I P L E S

111

1. C O U N C I L
2. A L A B A S T E R
3. D E L I G H T
4. M A R R I A G E
5. T E A C H E R
6. A B O M I N A T I O N
7. W O M A N
8. F I R M
9. H A P P E N E D
10. R U M O R

No greater than these, to love God and your neighbor. C O M M A N D M E N T S

112

1. L O U D E R
2. A R M E D
3. C R U C I F I E D
4. B A R A B B A S
5. T E M P T A T I O N
6. C O U R T Y A R D
7. A N O T H E R
8. P A S S O V E R
9. K I N G D O M
10. G U A R D E D

"The soldiers led Jesus away into the palace (that is, the P R A E T O R I U M) and called together the whole company of soldiers."

113

1. L O W B O R N
2. P E R S O N
3. V I C T O R Y
4. I N C R E A S E
5. B A L A N C E
6. S T O L E N
7. S H O U T
8. S A L V A T I O N
9. S A N D A L

"I have seen you in the S A N C T U A R Y and beheld your power and your glory."

114

1. B E H E A D E D
2. L O U D L Y
3. B E G G E D
4. P R I S O N
5. S U F F E R I N G
6. P A R A B L E
7. S Q U A L L
8. B R A N C H E S

No longer your own person. P O S S E S S E D

115

1. S T R U G G L I N G
2. C O V E T
3. B A P T I S M
4. T R A N S G R E S S
5. G R A C E
6. L A W F U L
7. R E P E N T
8. P R O M I S E

"You see, at just the right time, when we were still P O W E R L E S S, Christ died for the ungodly."

116

1. O F F S P R I N G
2. C O D E
3. C I R C U M C I S E
4. E N T R U S T E D
5. N A T U R E
6. G R U D G E
7. C R E D I T E D
8. W A V E R
9. O B L I G A T I O N
10. R E L E A S E D

"For if, when we were God's enemies, we were R E C O N C I L E D to him through the death of his Son, how much more, having been reconciled, shall we be saved through his life!"

117

1. P̲L̲A̲N̲N̲E̲D̲
2. S̲U̲M̲M̲O̲N̲
3. D̲E̲F̲I̲L̲E̲D̲
4. V̲I̲O̲L̲A̲T̲E̲
5. B̲R̲O̲K̲E̲N̲
6. C̲O̲N̲S̲U̲M̲E̲
7. E̲A̲R̲T̲H̲
8. D̲I̲S̲G̲R̲A̲C̲E̲
9. C̲O̲N̲S̲O̲L̲E̲

"The earth will be completely laid waste and totally PLUNDERED. The LORD has spoken this word."

118

1. J̲U̲D̲G̲I̲N̲G̲
2. T̲O̲U̲C̲H̲E̲D̲
3. R̲E̲G̲I̲O̲N̲
4. S̲T̲E̲R̲N̲L̲Y̲
5. I̲N̲D̲O̲O̲R̲S̲
6. E̲N̲T̲E̲R̲T̲A̲I̲N̲
7. N̲O̲I̲S̲Y̲
8. W̲I̲N̲E̲S̲K̲I̲N̲
9. C̲A̲R̲R̲Y̲
10. P̲R̲A̲C̲T̲I̲C̲E̲

He speaks to His angels CONCERNING us, for our sake.

119

1. F̲O̲O̲L̲I̲S̲H̲
2. P̲A̲R̲A̲L̲Y̲T̲I̲C̲
3. L̲A̲U̲G̲H̲E̲D̲
4. A̲M̲A̲Z̲E̲D̲
5. R̲E̲B̲U̲K̲E̲D̲
6. M̲E̲R̲C̲Y̲
7. H̲A̲R̲V̲E̲S̲T̲
8. S̲P̲R̲E̲A̲D̲

" 'Settle matters quickly with your ADVERSARY who is taking you to court.' "

120

1. B̲L̲E̲S̲S̲E̲D̲
2. P̲E̲R̲S̲E̲C̲U̲T̲E̲
3. R̲E̲J̲O̲I̲C̲E̲
4. W̲I̲N̲N̲O̲W̲
5. I̲N̲S̲U̲L̲T̲
6. P̲R̲O̲P̲H̲E̲T̲
7. M̲O̲U̲T̲H̲

" 'If SOMEONE forces you to go one mile, go with him two miles.' "

121

1. B̲L̲A̲S̲P̲H̲E̲M̲Y̲
2. G̲N̲A̲S̲H̲I̲N̲G̲
3. S̲O̲W̲E̲D̲
4. P̲E̲A̲R̲L̲
5. A̲M̲O̲U̲N̲T̲
6. H̲I̲D̲D̲E̲N̲
7. A̲R̲R̲I̲V̲E̲S̲
8. P̲E̲R̲C̲E̲I̲V̲E̲
9. C̲A̲R̲E̲L̲E̲S̲S̲
10. W̲I̲T̲H̲E̲R̲

" 'So when you give to the needy, do not announce it with trumpets, as the HYPOCRITES do in the synagogues and on the streets, to be honored by men.' "

122

1. C̲O̲N̲T̲R̲I̲T̲E̲
2. F̲L̲O̲U̲R̲I̲S̲H̲
3. M̲E̲M̲O̲R̲I̲A̲L̲
4. D̲E̲L̲I̲G̲H̲T̲
5. H̲I̲D̲D̲E̲N̲
6. A̲B̲U̲N̲D̲A̲N̲C̲E̲
7. W̲O̲R̲T̲H̲Y̲
8. L̲E̲V̲I̲T̲E̲
9. E̲X̲T̲E̲N̲D̲
10. S̲L̲A̲I̲N̲

"Behold, I will create new HEAVENS and a NEW earth. The former things will not be remembered, nor will they come to mind."

123

1. L̲O̲O̲S̲E̲D̲
2. C̲H̲I̲L̲D̲R̲E̲N̲
3. B̲R̲O̲T̲H̲E̲R̲
4. W̲I̲L̲L̲I̲N̲G̲
5. W̲A̲N̲D̲E̲R̲
6. P̲A̲G̲A̲N̲
7. B̲O̲U̲N̲D̲
8. B̲R̲I̲G̲H̲T̲L̲Y̲

" 'And when you pray, do not keep on BABBLING like pagans, for they think they will be heard because of their many words.' "

124

1. J̲O̲Y̲F̲U̲L̲
2. F̲A̲S̲T̲I̲N̲G̲
3. T̲R̲O̲U̲B̲L̲E̲
4. T̲H̲E̲R̲E̲F̲O̲R̲E̲
5. S̲A̲W̲D̲U̲S̲T̲
6. G̲L̲O̲R̲Y̲
7. R̲I̲G̲H̲T̲L̲Y̲
8. D̲E̲S̲P̲I̲S̲E̲

" 'When you fast, do not look somber as the hypocrites do, for they DISFIGURE their faces to show men they are fasting.' "

125

1. S̲P̲L̲E̲N̲D̲O̲R̲
2. G̲E̲N̲E̲R̲A̲T̲I̲O̲N̲
3. D̲O̲M̲I̲N̲I̲O̲N̲
4. M̲U̲S̲I̲C̲
5. M̲E̲D̲I̲T̲A̲T̲E̲
6. L̲A̲S̲T̲I̲N̲G̲
7. S̲H̲E̲P̲H̲E̲R̲D̲
8. C̲A̲L̲L̲E̲D̲

" 'But everyone who hears these words of mine and does not put them into PRACTICE is like a foolish man who built his house on sand.' "

126

1. W̲I̲T̲N̲E̲S̲S̲
2. D̲A̲U̲G̲H̲T̲E̲R̲
3. R̲E̲S̲C̲U̲E̲
4. C̲O̲U̲N̲T̲R̲Y̲
5. S̲A̲N̲H̲E̲D̲R̲I̲N̲
6. E̲G̲Y̲P̲T̲
7. F̲A̲M̲I̲N̲E̲
8. P̲E̲R̲F̲O̲R̲M̲

The members of the Synagogue of the FREEDMEN opposed Stephen.

127

1. P O I S O N
2. S N A R E
3. B A T T L E
4. W O V E N
5. S L A N D E R
6. S U R R O U N D
7. A D V E R S A R Y

"The LORD will fulfill his purpose for me; your love, O LORD, endures forever—do not A B A N D O N the works of your hands."

128

1. F I R S T B O R N
2. E N T H R O N E D
3. A B U N D A N T
4. W O N D E R S
5. P R O V I S I O N
6. U N F A I L I N G
7. P R O S P E R I T Y
8. P R A I S E

"When I was in distress, I sought the Lord; at night I stretched out U N T I R I N G hands and my soul refused to be comforted."

129

1. S W E R V I N G
2. P A R C H E D
3. F O R C E S
4. B U R N E D
5. J E A L O U S
6. N O R T H E R N
7. J O S T L E

"The word of the LORD that came to Joel son of P E T H U E L."

130

1. W R I T T E N
2. G E N T I L E S
3. R E P U T E D
4. S L A V E R Y
5. B A R R E N
6. Z E A L O U S
7. P U R P O S E
8. S P I R I T
9. G A L A T I A N S
10. G O S P E L

"Now that faith has come, we are no longer under the S U P E R V I S I O N of the law."

131

1. D I S C E R N
2. F O L L Y
3. F A T T E N E D
4. C A L M S
5. S H A M E F U L
6. T R U T H F U L
7. M O C K E R
8. S U B J E C T

" 'At that time,' D E C L A R E S the LORD, 'I will be the God of all the clans of Israel, and they will be my people.' "

132

1. P L E A S E S
2. H A U G H T Y
3. O B T A I N
4. C O N S I D E R
5. S E C R E T
6. S O O T H E S
7. W E A L T H
8. H U N G R Y
9. R E P R O A C H

Jeremiah tells of a time when the people of God will be A B H O R R E N T to all the kingdoms of the earth.

133

1. H O L I N E S S
2. P R I S O N
3. P E A C E
4. D E S T I T U T E
5. H E A L E D
6. O U T C O M E
7. I M I T A T E
8. D I S G R A C E
9. E N J O Y
10. I S A A C

"It is good for our hearts to be strengthened by grace, not by C E R E M O N I A L foods, which are of no value to those who eat them."

134

1. P U R P O S E
2. B R I B E
3. J U S T I C E
4. P A C I F I E S
5. U P M O S T
6. T E R R O R
7. G R A V E L
8. K N O W L E D G E

A M I R A C U L O U S catch of fish.

135

1. T R I U M P H A L
2. D I S C I P L E S
3. D E N A R I U S
4. P R E P A R E
5. G R E A T
6. T E A C H E R
7. M A S T E R
8. T R I B E S
9. P R O P H E T

On the way to Jerusalem, Jesus and His disciples came to B E T H P H A G E on the Mount of Olives.

136

1. G R I E V O U S
2. P E O P L E
3. B E N E F I T
4. M E A N I N G
5. E X T R E M E
6. S T R A N G E R
7. A V O I D
8. D E L I G H T

They spoke of a new covenant. M I N I S T E R S

188

137

1. A C T I O N S
2. B O A S T I N G
3. F O R E V E R
4. A C T I V I T I E S
5. I N F E R I O R
6. P R E T E N D
7. F A L S E
8. W E A K L I N G

"For you were once
D A R K N E S S, but now you are
light in the Lord. Live as children of light."

138

1. D I S C R E T I O N
2. S T R A I G H T
3. H I G H W A Y
4. E X A L T
5. T E M P E R E D
6. T H O R N S
7. R E P O S E
8. P R U D E N T

"Dishonest money D W I N D L E S
away, but he who gathers money little by little
makes it grow."

139

1. T O N G U E
2. W O U N D S
3. P A T I E N C E
4. G E N T L E
5. F O O L I S H
6. E N V I O U S
7. P O V E R T Y
8. S L U G G A R D
9. B O A S T
10. Q U A R R E L

"Like a madman shooting
F I R E B R A N D S or
deadly arrows is a man who deceives his neighbor
and says, 'I was only joking!' "

140

1. L O N G I N G
2. R A S H L Y
3. S E A R C H E S
4. U P R O O T E D
5. T H R E A T
6. R E S C U E D
7. C R U E L

"A fool shows his annoyance at once, but a
P R U D E N T man overlooks an
insult."

141

1. B A N I S H
2. C A P T I V E
3. C O N T E M P T
4. R I D I C U L E
5. B U I L D E R
6. R E T U R N
7. D E C R E E
8. L O F T Y

"Save me, O Lord, from lying lips and from
D E C E I T F U L tongues."

142

1. W A S T E L A N D
2. W I T H H E L D
3. F E A T H E R S
4. H A S T E
5. P R O V I D E
6. M E A D O W
7. C L O T H E D
8. P R O C L A I M

God puts the lonely in
F A M I L I E S.

143

1. S H E A T H E D
2. C H E R I S H
3. A C C O M P A N Y
4. S C A T T E R
5. D W E L L I N G
6. R E F U G E
7. F A L L E N
8. F I L L E D

"A father to the fatherless, a
D E F E N D E R of widows,
is God in his holy dwelling."

144

1. S T R I P P E D
2. B A R E F O O T
3. O F F I C I A L S
4. E S C A P E
5. D O N K E Y S
6. S T R A N G E
7. F I G H T
8. I D O L S

"An oracle concerning Arabia: You caravans of
D E D A N I T E S, who camp in
the thickets of Arabia."

145

1. L O D G E
2. M A N G L E S
3. D E M A N D
4. B E T H L E H E M
5. B E C A U S E
6. G L E A N
7. K I N G S H I P
8. C R U S H

"Listen to what the Lord says: 'Stand up, plead
your case before the
M O U N T A I N S; let the hills
hear what you have to say.' "

146

1. G O O D W I L L
2. T R A P P E D
3. D E C E I T
4. G A T H E R S
5. P R E T E N D
6. A D V I C E
7. P E R I S H
8. B E N E F I T

"The sluggard craves and gets nothing, but the
desires of the D I L I G E N T
are fully satisfied."

147

1. J E S U S
2. P R O P H E T S
3. S H A D O W S
4. S A N D A L
5. B A P T I Z E
6. N A P H T A L I
7. P A R A B L E
8. S P I R I T
9. P H A R I S E E S
10. B E A T I T U D E S
11. S A L T

He really lost his head over Jesus. Who was he?

J O H N the B A P T I S T

148

1. P E R S E V E R E
2. P A G A N S
3. B R O T H E R
4. R E V E L A T I O N
5. S I N S
6. F U L L N E S S
7. F E L L O W S H I P

This church had a golden lampstand named after it.

E P H E S U S

149

1. P E O P L E
2. G R O A N I N G
3. C O N S I D E R
4. S O V E R E I G N
5. M E R C Y
6. S I N F U L
7. S T R U G G L E
8. C O N T R O L
9. P A S S I O N S

She may have had the same name, but she was not the wife of the famous singer. Who was she?

P R I S C I L L A

150

1. B A P T I Z E
2. W O N D E R
3. S O R C E R Y
4. Y O U T H
5. D E C L A R E
6. S T R I C K E N
7. M U L T I P L Y
8. E A R T H
9. H A N D S

This prophet was the son of Berekiah.

Z E C H A R I A H

151

1. P E O P L E
2. G R E A T
3. I N C R E A S E
4. R E S T O R E
5. D E V O U R
6. O U T C A S T
7. B E H O L D
8. P A S S
9. S M I T E

Such a wind was worth the wait.

P E N T E C O S T

152

1. N E A R
2. G R E E N
3. S I E G E
4. R U L E R S
5. G I R D L E S
6. S I S T E R
7. D E R I S I O N
8. C O N T A I N
9. S C A T T E R
10. P I T Y
11. H O U S E
12. H E A T H E N

What is it that all believers will experience?

R E S U R R E C T I O N

153

1. B L E S S E D
2. S P I R I T
3. M O U R N
4. F O R B A D E
5. P I N N A C L E

He threw a party for Jesus, but was not prepared for the woman with the perfume.

S I M O N

154

1. R E V I L E
2. G A L I L E E
3. T E M P L E
4. C O U N T R Y
5. A N G E L
6. H E A R D
7. R E J O I C E
8. H E R O D
9. P R I S O N
10. P E A R L
11. B L A D E

Who is like the greatest in heaven?

L I T T L E   C H I L D

155

1. J E S U S
2. D A M S E L
3. D E P A R T
4. T I M E
5. R E C E I V E
6. H O N O R
7. K I N G D O M

Many feet meant a dramatic change for this place.

J E R I C H O

156

1. S A I L E D
2. N A T U R E
3. S L O T H
4. G I V E N
5. S N A R E
6. C O N T E M P T
7. I N T R E A T
8. P R I N C E
9. G R A S S

Many who had an important job to do for the Lord received this first. What was it?

A N O I N T I N G

157
1. (Z) I D O N
2. B A T T L E
3. R I S I N G
4. T R I B E (S)
5. P L A I N S
6. S T R E N G T (H)
7. C H (A) R I O T S
8. (T O) W A R D
9. D E A T (H)

This town was home to a widow and her son who were very glad to have Elijah stay with them.
(Z) (A) (R) (E) (P) (H) (A) (T) (H)

158
1. A B O V (E)
2. (Z) A C C U R
3. J U D G M (E) N T
4. W O R (K) M A N
5. W (I) L L I N G
6. S E R V I C (E)
7. B O W (L) S

Wheels and scrolls—a vision for this prophet. Who was he?
(E) (Z) (E) (K) (I) (E) (L)

159
1. J O (B)
2. (A) P P O I N T E D
3. T R O O (P) S
4. (T) E R R O R S
5. P (I) L L A R S
6. (Z) E B E D E E
7. E X A L T (E) D

In the old days, a little water would clean one right up!
(B) (A) (P) (T) (I) (Z) (E)

160
1. C O N S U M (E)
2. E (X) A L T
3. (P) L E A S U R E
4. S E R V (A) N T
5. A (N) S W E R
6. W O R (S) H I P
7. P A S T U R (E)

In the beginning, there was nothing to separate water until God created it. What was it?
(E) (X) (P) (A) (N) (S) (E)

161
1. E (A) T E N
2. (B) O N E S
3. T E R R I B L E
4. H E (A) R T H
5. R I G (H) T E O U S
6. O R D I N (A) N C E
7. E N E (M) Y

This righteous man had a difficult time with fear.
(A) (B) (R) (A) (H) (A) (M)

162
1. (J) E R E M I A H
2. T R O (U) B L E
3. S P E A K
4. N E I T (H) E R
5. B U (I) L D
6. T (A) R S H I S H

This son of Nun took control of a nation.
(J) (O) (S) (H) (U) (A)

163
1. W I L D E (R) N E S S
2. C O U N T R Y
3. W H E A (T)
4. W E I G (H) T
5. R E M E M (B) E R
6. L (O) R D
7. B R (A) C E L E T
8. (Z) I O N

This couple fell in love on a threshing floor.
(R) (U) (T) (H) and (B) (O) (A) (Z)

164
1. (G) R E A T
2. H (O) R S E S
3. J E A L (O) U S
4. M (I) D S T
5. J E R U S (A) L E M
6. P L U M M E (T)
7. (H) O S T S

He should have ducked. Who was he?
(G) (O) (L) (I) (A) (T) (H)

165
1. (S) I N F U L
2. F (A) T H E R
3. A S S E M B L (E)
4. (V) I S I O N
5. G L A D N E S S
6. B R E T (H) R E N
7. F A (I) T H
8. (O) P E N E D
9. F O U (N) D

Whom shall we fear when the Lord is our light and our. . . ?
(S) (A) (L) (V) (A) (T) (I) (O) (N)

166
1. (S) A M A R I A
2. R E M (O) V E
3. S E P U L (C) H R E
4. A N (O) I N T E D
5. B E T H L E H E (M)
6. C (O) V E N A N T
7. C A P T A I (N)

He made the right choice and was blessed more than any other man.
(S) (O) (L) (O) (M) (O) (N)

167

1. D(E)L I V E R
2. P R E (S) E N C E
3. C E R (T) A I N
4. (H)E A V E N
5. F I (E) L D S
6. P (R) A I S E

She became queen and saved Israel. Who was she?
(E)(S)(T)(H)(E)(R)

168

1. L A M (E) N T
2. S E R V I (C) E
3. (C) O M E
4. B E H O L D
5. T W E N T Y
6. F O R S A K E
7. B U I L D
8. D E P A R T
9. S O U L
10. H A S T E
11. V A L L E Y
12. S E R V A N T S

This book of the Bible is good for learning.
(E)(C)(C)(L)(E)(S)(I)(A)(S)(T)(E)(S)

169

1. (P) O R T E R
2. W I (T) N E S S
3. D I S C I P (L) E
4. S (A) V E D
5. F A (T) H E R
6. S T R A N G (E) R

He asked Jesus if He was the King of the Jews.
(P)(I)(L)(A)(T)(E)

170

1. H U N D R E (D)
2. T R (E) E S
3. C H E R U (B) I M
4. H (O) U S E
5. G (R) O U N D
6. M E (A) S U R E S
7. A R C (H) E S

She was a female judge who ruled Israel.
(D)(E)(B)(O)(R)(A)(H)

171

1. T H I N (K)
2. (N) A T I O N S
3. G R (O) W
4. S P A R R O (W) S
5. L I L I E S
6. R A V E (N) S
7. (D) E L A Y
8. (G) R A V E S
9. S C R I B (E) S

Charity edifies, but this puffs up. What is it?
(K)(N)(O)(W)(L)(E)(D)(G)(E)

172

1. (G) L O R Y
2. (M) A N N E R
3. W A (L) K
4. (A) N G E L
5. P R I V A (T) E
6. P R O M (I) S E
7. P (R) A Y I N G
8. A C C O U (N) T
9. P L E A S (E)

Who were the people who were bewitched?
(G)(A)(L)(A)(T)(I)(A)(N)(S)

173

1. E N (T) E R
2. T (I) T H E S
3. I N F I R (M) I T I E S
4. D (O) C T R I N E
5. M (O) T H E R
6. (H) O L Y
7. F O R T (Y)

Who was Paul's own son in the faith?
(T)(I)(M)(O)(T)(H)(Y)

174

1. F (L) E S H
2. L I B E R T (Y)
3. W R (I) T T E N
4. U (N) D E R
5. (G) R A C E
6. B E S T O (W) E D
7. A L L E G (O) R Y
8. S I (N) A I
9. B O N (D) A G E
10. L (E) A V E N
11. C H (R) I S T
12. (S) E A S O N

Satan comes with all power, signs, and what else?
(L)(Y)(I)(N)(G) (W)(O)(N)(D)(E)(R)(S)

175

1. S T R E N G T (H)
2. D O M (I) N I O N
3. (S) A I N T S
4. B (R) E A D T H
5. P O W (E) R
6. (W) I S H F U L
7. G (A) T H E R
8. W (R) A T H
9. P R U (D) E N C E

What is a laborer worthy of?
(H)(I)(S) (R)(E)(W)(A)(R)(D)